# the Promise of Purpose

PROVEN STRATEGIES TO REACH
YOUR GOD-GIVEN POTENTIAL

# the *Promise* of *Purpose*

## KAREN CONRAD

Harrison House
Shippensburg, PA

Published by Harrison House Publishers
Shippensburg, PA 17257

Cover design by Eileen Rockwell

ISBN 13 TP: 978-1-6803-1767-1

ISBN 13 eBook: 978-1-6803-1766-4

ISBN 13 HC: 978-1-6803-1769-5

ISBN 13 LP: 978-1-6803-1768-8

For Worldwide Distribution, Printed in the USA

1  2  3  4  5  6  7  8 / 25  24  23  22  21

# Contents

# Introduction

All my life, I was the one who jumped out of bed in the morning, ready to take on whatever the day would bring. I was not a Pollyanna, believing everything was storybook perfect. I was fully aware there would be challenges and difficulties, but I appreciated a challenge and relished the feeling of accomplishment that came with a resolution. I had actually been nicknamed the Energizer Bunny more than once.

Then, I took a new job. It was an excellent promotion, included a pay raise, and was a significant leadership role. Imagine how confusing and disorienting it was when, after one month, I could no longer drag myself out of bed. Bouncing out of bed ready for the day was not only out of the question, it was impossible. I couldn't rouse myself enough to arrive at a meeting destination forty minutes away until I was actually scheduled to be there. I couldn't make myself care about being over an hour late, even though I was the boss. I spent my lunch hours weeping uncontrollably, often lamenting to the Lord and trying to figure out what was wrong with me.

What could possibly have happened between the job I had loved and held for over thirteen years and this new position? I had spent a great deal of time praying and asking the Lord for guidance before leaving my previous position. After seeking godly counsel, I felt I heard the Lord say, "You are free to take the new job." What was the problem? What was I doing wrong?

After three months of torturously dragging myself through life, it felt as though I was on the verge of a breakdown. One day after sharing these issues with my dad, he said, "Karen, maybe you just need to quit." His words were empathetic and reassuring. They provided the confidence I needed to act. Immediately, I felt the Lord release me to hand in my resignation. I heard Him say, "Karen, you have one chance to be a mom. I will restore your career." That was the beginning of the greatest adventure I have lived so far in my life.

My son, Levi, was sixteen years old when my husband, Levi's father, died suddenly and without any warning. Levi and I had spent the following two years after his death just surviving, but we were beginning to feel ourselves break through the waves that had threatened to overcome us. God had been and was continuing to be faithful, and we held on to Him literally for our lives.

Now two years after that trauma, Levi was close to graduating from high school and was preparing to attend a university in the fall. I submitted my resignation at my new job and said goodbye to my colleagues with no clarity on what the future would hold. I had God's Word and set out to discover what He had purposed for me. I spent my mornings praying and reading the Word and the afternoons exploring Minnesota with Levi by my side. I wanted to maximize our time together, as we talked in depth about life, what we were learning, and our hopes and dreams.

My episode with despair and hopelessness could very well be explained as a stage of grief, fear, or even depression, but the important thing for me was not so much what it was but what it did. It was the catalyst that caused me to dig deep into God's Word and find out who He said I was. I discovered that He saw me and knew me, and He had created me for a purpose. I can't tell you there was the flip of a switch and everything in my life was all good. I have found that God rarely uses the flip of a switch or snap of a finger—an instant change—because He knows us so well. We need the process. We thrive on the journey, and He adds so much to us along the way. In my experience, the journey can be even more important than the destination.

During this time, I learned that God sees us in our place of hurt. He lovingly finds us and speaks to our destiny and purpose. Like a good shepherd, God not only sees but guides. He watches over us with eyes of grace and compassion to guide us into our purpose. I was recently reminded of the story of Hagar in the book of Genesis where this exact thing happened. The story describes how God sees Hagar in a place of vulnerability and despair and speaks to her purpose.

To give context to the story of Hagar, in Genesis chapter 12 God speaks to a man named Abram. At the age of seventy-five, God tells Abram to leave his land behind and travel to a new, undisclosed geographical location. God promised that Abram would be blessed, and he and his wife, Sarai, would have a child. This promised child would grow into a great nation, and his descendants would outnumber the sand of the seashore. Abram and Sarai tried for ten years to fulfill God's promise of conceiving and bearing a child.

In Genesis chapter 16, the story involving Hagar starts to unfold. Sarai lost hope in the promise as she watched year after year pass with no child. She became frustrated and crafted an idea for Abram to sleep with Hagar, her Egyptian slave. Sarai planned to build a family through her. Sarai communicated this idea to Abram, who agreed, and she gave Hagar to her husband, Abram, as a wife. He slept with Hagar, and she conceived. Abram would finally have an heir; a son would be born to fulfill God's promise. However, within a short period of time, the plan began to unravel. Hagar despised Sarai. Sarai went to Abram and blamed him for the relational difficulty she was enduring. Abram told Sarai to do whatever she thought was best, and Sarai mistreated Hagar until she left their household and hid in the desert.

Hagar shifted from being Abram's wife and the mother of his child to being unwanted and pressured to leave. In the desert, the angel of the Lord appeared to her as she sat beside a spring of water. This was the first time the angel of the Lord appeared in the Bible. He is the pre-incarnate Jesus, Yeshua, the same angel of the Lord who later wrestles with Jacob. He came to save Hagar, the grandmother of the Arab nation. He asked her, "Where have you come from and where are you going?" (Gen. 16:8, ESV). This question is similar to the question asked in the Passover Exodus story, where God brought the Israelites out of Egypt to safety. He was asking her where she has been brought out of. It speaks of her life story and identity. Second, He wanted to know where she was going because He wanted to address her future. Hagar had no vision for her future, and God wanted her to see she had a purpose. He told her she was pregnant with a son, and she was to name him Ishmael, meaning, "the Lord hears." God gave Hagar vision and purpose for her life.

Based on her encounter, Hagar called God *El Rohee*, or "You are the God who sees me." She named the place of her encounter "the well of the Living One who sees me." She said, "Truly here I have seen him who looks after me" (Gen. 16:13, ESV). God revealed in this situation something important for all of us to understand. God sees you. He intimately loves and cares about you. He has a purpose for your life. You will have challenges and difficult circumstances that will feel insurmountable, but God sees you and is present to guide you through to your purpose.

This book is a compilation of the beautiful truths the Lord has made real in my life since the day I discovered He sees me and knows me. He was working in and through me even before I knew it. He was preparing me for what was ahead in my life. I will tell you about finding my life purpose—seeing vision come to reality. I will show you how my life message—we are uniquely created and gifted for a purpose—changed my life. I am beyond excited to help you discover your purpose and vision and lead you on a path to making it a reality.

I invite you to take this journey with me. My prayer as you read this book is that God will reveal how He has created you for a purpose and what that purpose is. I have provided tools for discovering your purpose and walking into your success. You will gain practical methods for stepping into your purpose with courage and confidence. I will share processes the Lord gave me to combat fear and limitations.

The conclusion of each chapter will include an Activations section to help you process the information within the chapter on a personal level and apply it to your life. You are in for a journey that will change your life. This great adventure of discovering your destiny will reveal how to live a life overflowing with the joy and success Jesus has provided for you. I pray you will find your unique place as you begin to understand His purpose for your life.

Chapter One

# You Were Made for a Purpose

I t seemed I had spent a lifetime trying to achieve success, but I was always falling short in some way. I was never good enough to say, "I made it." No matter how hard I worked (and I worked hard) or how many achievements I made along the way, something would always set me back to square one. *Is this what life was supposed to be?* I often wondered. *Success based on my latest achievements, relationships, and finances being faultless?* Failure was always just ahead, as I didn't measure up to my own high standards and expectations.

The disapproval of those I cared about pleasing, such as my family, boss, or colleagues, produced an endless cycle of self-criticism and disappointment. Rejection had become my middle name. My emotions had become a roller coaster of highs and lows, depending on my latest achievement or failure, which produced anxiety at every level. All of this combined with a traumatic event, and my life looked like a recipe for disaster.

My personal anxiety stemmed from an atmosphere of fear, including the fear of rejection, the fear of man, and the fear of failure. I can't tell you where it all started, but I can tell you it affected me

# God has created you with an incredible, personal and unique purpose.

in every area of my life. I needed God to intervene, and He did in a very unexpected way. I still remember, as if it was yesterday, driving home from a meeting that had gone wrong. I admit I was crying out in anger toward God from frustration and defeat. I had shared some ideas, which I was certain God had given me, with my leadership, only to have them rejected and dismissed. Through anger and tears, my conversation with God went something like, "God, why did You call me here if no one appreciates what I bring to the table?" I was certain that the Lord had me move across the country for this job, so I didn't understand what was happening. I was mad. I was hurt. And, I was feeling the all-too-familiar pain of failure and rejection once again.

What came next changed my life. In a gentle, loving voice, I heard in my heart, "Karen, the gifts and talents you have are from Me." My initial reaction was to retort, "I know that!" After all, I had read the Bible! But the gentle voice came again, "No, Karen…the gifts and talents you have are Mine, and I have placed them in you to help you fulfill the purpose I have designed for your life. It's more important to Me than to you that *My* gifts and talents are honored."

A weight came off of me in that moment. For the first time in my life, I understood that I didn't have to fight for people's approval of me or my work. God wanted to take responsibility for that area in my life—if I'd let Him. I had been unknowingly taking ownership of the gifts and talents God had so graciously given me. I had taken full responsibility for producing favorable results rather than living in a stewardship role. It was an exhausting way to live, and I was ready to make a change. God had just empowered me to "get over myself."

I spent the following days and weeks seeking God on what this all meant. I recounted the words He had spoken to my heart, and one phrase continued to stand out: "the gifts and talents you have are Mine, and I have placed them in you to help you fulfill the purpose I have designed for your life." *Purpose.* I had found the key to unlock true success and unleash my God-given destiny that day, but I still had a lot to learn. I began fervently seeking God on the meaning of purpose, how to discover His purpose for my life, and how to fulfill that purpose. I knew true satisfaction and success would flow from understanding and walking out my purpose with Him.

## *I had found the key to unlock true success and unleash my God-given destiny that day.*

So, where do we begin? How about with God's definition of *purpose.*

*Purpose* is God's display to the world of His workmanship in you. Your purpose was uniquely designed by God. You have a future that He wants to reveal and open up before you. All you have to do is choose to cooperate with His process and provision to help you achieve your God-given destiny. The apostle Paul explains God's intentional design for you and your life of purpose: "For we are his workmanship, created in Christ Jesus for good works, which God prepared beforehand, that we should walk in them" (Eph. 2:10, ESV). Your salvation comes by grace, through faith. Once saved, you co-labor with God and achieve (serve) by doing those good works He intended for you.

Paul describes specific elements related to your purpose. First, you are unique, a result of God's intentional design and plan. God purposely thought about you and wrote the intimate details of your formation in His book, the Bible. He then formed you according to His plan while you were in your mother's womb. God was present at your birth, and your days were actively planned. In Psalm 139:16, David wrote, "Your eyes have seen my unformed substance; and in Your book were all written the days that were ordained for me, when as yet there was not one of them" (NASB95). David went on to say, "Your thoughts are far beyond my understanding, much more than I could ever imagine. I try to count your thoughts, but they outnumber the grains of sand on the beach. And when I awake, I will find you nearby" (Ps. 139:17-18, CEV). The beach is enjoyable, with its views, warmth, the sound of waves, and sense of relaxation. It's a place of inspiration for me as I experience God's beauty. When I glance down at the sand, it's almost overwhelming to think that God's precious thoughts of me outnumber those grains of sand.

You are created in Jesus for good works. When you became born again, you became a new creation, transformed by Jesus. You now have specific divine attributes, rights, and opportunities. Your priority is a relationship with God, and what you do in life flows from that. God purposely designed you, and out of that heavenly design, He planned and prepared your life for achievement. He has positioned you to succeed in your purpose with His loving help.

An example of this can be found in Exodus 31:3. God anointed Bezalel as a skilled craftsman for the purpose of working on the Tabernacle. God said, "I have filled him with the Spirit of God, in wisdom, and in understanding, and in knowledge, and in all manner of workmanship" (KJV). Moses received the instructions to build the Tabernacle, but God gave Bezalel the purpose to do the work. Walking in your purpose is part of God's good works He has prepared for you.

The activities of your life are a form of worship to bring attention to God's greatness and His goodness. Again, Paul describes this well in Colossians 3:23, "Put your heart and soul into every activity you do, as though you are doing it for the Lord himself and not merely for others" (TPT). You are God's garden and God's building. He has given you the grace to do what He has called you to do. It's a special endowment of grace for your task or purpose. Grace is God's ability, strength, and power at work in you. God gives you favor that enables you to do and be everything He says you can do and be. God's grace comes to you unmerited. He has already done everything by grace for you, and you have already received it into your born-again spirit. He has given you every spiritual blessing, and faith is simply your reaction to Him. By faith, you reach into the spirit realm and receive what God has already given you.

Paul wrote, "For we are God's fellow workers; you are God's field, you are God's building. According to the grace of God which was given to me, as a wise master builder I have laid the foundation, and another builds on it. But let each one take heed how he builds on it. For no other foundation can anyone lay than that which is laid, which is Jesus Christ" (1 Cor. 3:9-11, NKJV). Paul said there is no foundation other than Jesus Christ. God laid the foundation, which is

Christ, and He completes the foundational work in you. And before the foundation of the world, He equipped you for your purpose. He partners with you for success.

Are you under the impression you don't have gifts or talents? Do you feel that God hasn't given what you need to succeed? Those are lies. You can get that out of your thinking completely and hold on to this beautiful verse: "As each one has received a special gift, employ it in serving one another as good stewards of the multifaceted grace of God" (1 Pet. 4:10, NASB). The Amplified Bible further defines "special gift" as "a spiritual talent, an ability graciously given by God." You can be assured that He has given and you have received a special gift, a spiritual talent, an ability graciously given by God. Use it!

*The gifts and talents He's given you are perfectly designed for you. Just relax.*

Sometimes you may feel as though you want to be like other people. Be aware that it's a terrible waste of time and energy to compare ourselves with others. God gave your gifts to you and their gifts to them. The Amplified version of 1 Peter 4:10 says that God has given us "diverse, varied gifts and abilities." We must stop looking at what other people are doing and instead seek God on what we've been called to do. Coveting someone else's gifts and talents won't help us discover ours.

THE PROMISE OF PURPOSE

Once you seek Him and learn what it is you're called to do, that grace reservoir of gifts and talents will be revealed. Isn't this getting exciting?

The gifts and talents He's given you are perfectly designed for you. Just relax. Your gifts and talents are from God and for His purpose, so you can rest, knowing He values what He has given to you. In his book, James said that "Every good thing given and every perfect gift is from above, coming down from the Father of lights, with whom there is no variation or shifting shadow" (James 1:17, NASB). I am so encouraged by this verse. The gifts He has put in me are good, perfect, and from Him. I have been given gifts from the Father of lights! There is no reason to fear being overlooked or undervalued. He wants to see those gifts and talents used for His Kingdom and acknowledged with value even more than you do. And He promises to bring you the increase: "I planted, Apollos watered, but God gave the increase. So then neither he who plants is anything, nor he who waters, but God who gives the increase" (1 Cor. 3:6-7, NKJV).

Do you wonder sometimes what the Lord thinks about you or how He sees you? God says that you are where you are on purpose, not by accident. He has appointed, placed, and purposefully planted you so your fruit will remain and be lasting. John said it this way: "You have not chosen Me, but I have chosen you and I have appointed and placed and purposefully planted you, so that you would go and bear fruit and keep on bearing, and that your fruit will remain and be lasting, so that whatever you ask of the Father in My name [as My representative] He may give to you" (John 15:16, AMP).

Whatever you ask in His name as His representative He *will* give you. When you look through the lens of your purpose, you can see yourself the way He sees you. And it's so good! As you understand and function in the gifts and talents God has given you, success comes supernaturally through Him. Your success is imminent when you're pursuing God in His purpose for your life: "Then Joshua said to the people, 'Sanctify yourselves [for His purpose], for tomorrow the Lord will do wonders (miracles) among you'" (Josh. 3:5, AMP). This verse starts by saying, "Sanctify yourselves [for His purpose]." What follows is the Lord doing wonders and miracles through and among them. *Sanctification* means to set apart. When we set ourselves apart, we separate ourselves from our daily concerns to seek and hear God. It's His voice that brings wisdom, comfort, and direction. How fabulous that God thinks you are a worthy bearer of His glory and wonder.

## *Is there more to life? You bet there is.*

God has pre-arranged a good life for you. He has not planned a bad life but a good life for you. Ephesians 2:10 tells us, "For we are His workmanship, created in Christ Jesus for good works, which God prepared beforehand that we should walk in them" (NKJV). He has provided everything you need to live the life He has made ready for you. He thinks very highly of you, He sees great things in you, and He gave you gifts because He trusts you. God has so much He wants to do through you. He loves you so much, and He has a beautiful life designed specifically for you. He wants you to enjoy your time on Earth and participate in having His kingdom come and His will be done in your life.

Eternity begins right here right now. Decide to live in His abundant life beginning today. "[Not in your own strength] for it is God Who is all the while effectually at work in you [energizing and creating in you the power and desire], both to will and to work for His good pleasure and satisfaction and delight" (Phil. 2:13, AMPC). Nothing is accomplished in your own strength. You are not strong enough to endure some of the things in your path. I certainly wasn't. Without Him, you are not equipped to accomplish the dreams in your heart. But when you get over yourself—stop relying on yourself—and decide to take Him at His Word, He can accomplish so much more. What a joy to walk through a day, knowing that God is effectually at work in you. He is energizing and creating in you the power and desire to do His will. He takes responsibility for everything. He knows everything you have been through, and He knows everything you can be.

Is there more to life? You bet there is. You were created for a unique purpose—beyond what you can accomplish in your own power. When you discover your purpose and connect to the plan God laid out for you from the foundation of the world, you'll experience satisfaction. Your gifts and talents from the Lord are designed specifically to give your life meaning and purpose. You were made for greatness!

## ACTIVATION

Write down your gifts and talents. Then, go through the list and thank the Lord for His creativity in the way He made you.

---

Ask the Lord to reveal to you various aspects of your life's purpose and communicate with Him concerning what He tells you.

Write out the dreams and passions you may have secretly held in your heart.

Living Your Purpose Download:

https://drive.google.com/file/d/1tzKqghPxJqP08v8S0s9gZqw9bjQ9_Txt/view?usp=sharing

Jesus came for you to have the quality of life He has—life abundant.

# Chapter Two

# Purpose Starts with a Heart-to-Heart Connection

I have taken a multitude of personality and strength locator tests over the years in an attempt to better understand how I think, what type of career I am best suited for, and in general how to be more successful. These types of assessments can be very helpful in understanding how to work better with others, but they didn't help me with the one question I was craving to have answered: Why am I here? It's a question I expect everyone has asked at one time or another, and perhaps you are asking it today.

When I graduated from college in December 1986, I began the process of looking for a professional job. I was interviewing for a sales job in a check printing company out of Shoreview, Minnesota. It would entail calling on banks throughout Minnesota and the Dakotas. I really wanted this job and had made it through multiple interviews. The last step in the interview process was to take a personality test to ensure I was a good fit. Taking the test was a fearful experience. I was going to pass or fail the job interview process based on my test results.

I wish I could tell you I passed with flying colors and got the job, but it was just the opposite. I received a rejection letter in the mail shortly after I had taken the test. I was devastated.

I had based my self-worth and identity on a foundation of being liked and accepted. When you do that, fear, failure and rejection are around every corner. I didn't have a solid foundation in Christ Jesus or my identity in Him. This experience revealed that my identity was built on shifting sand. I look back now, realizing I was so full of fear and anxiety, it probably came through loud and clear in the assessment. Unlocking your purpose begins with developing an intimate relationship with the Lord and establishing your identity in Him.

Let me reassure you. We all have a unique purpose, designed by God, and I am dedicated to helping you discover and develop that God-given purpose in order to achieve your full potential. That said, we also share a common purpose as sons and daughters of God, which is the foundation for unlocking your unique purpose and unleashing your destiny.

Where do we begin? The starting point for understanding the purpose for your life is to have a heart-to-heart connection and relationship with God. In that relationship, you will learn to understand the real you, based on who you are in Jesus. Your particular purpose is revealed and realized in your personal relationship with God. Everything springboards from there, and in this wonderful discovery process you will experience an amazing adventure with Him. In this chapter, we'll take a closer look at our relational foundation to understand how it is that we, together with God, discover and walk out our purpose and destiny.

I only ever knew myself based on others' opinions and through a lens of my past mistakes. I didn't know the real Karen based on what Jesus had done for me or through the lens in which He sees me. You see, the Holy Spirit guides you into truth so you can remove the restraining boundaries of yourself and open the doors to experience your best possible life. I hope you are gathering the principles and tools needed to unleash your destiny based on your heart-to-heart connection with God. His greatest desire is *you!*

*Once I became aware that He is in me and with me, I felt as though I had a new best friend!*

How do you develop this kind of relationship? I had been taught to spend time in my "prayer closet," which, to be candid, did not sound very appealing to me. Who wants to spend time in a closet? Is that where I have to go to communicate with God? If so, I wanted to get in and out as quickly as possible! But as I began to spend my mornings in the front room of my home, praying, studying the Word, and talking with God as if He was sitting on the couch with me, I quickly discovered how funny, adventurous, and personal God is. Once I let go of the religious ideas I had about praying and spending time with God and became aware that He is in me and with me, I felt as though I had a new best friend!

———

While reading one day, I noticed the apostle Paul, who I consider a superstar in ministry, said this in Philippians 3:10, "[For my determined purpose is] that I may know Him [that I may progressively become more deeply and intimately acquainted with Him, perceiving and recognizing and understanding the wonders of His Person more strongly and more clearly], and that I may in that same way come to know the power outflowing from His resurrection" (AMPC). Paul could have said so many things, such as, "My purpose is to write most of the New Testament or to preach to thousands." But he didn't say any of that. He said his determined purpose was to *know God,* and as a result he would come to know the power flowing from His resurrection. That rocked my world.

Paul recognized that his determined purpose in life was to know God personally and intimately, which is the foundational purpose in all our lives. With that as a foundation, he went on to accomplish amazing things through his own unique purpose, but he knew how to keep the main thing the main thing. You and I can learn from Paul. Your relationship with the Lord is the most important part of fulfilling your purpose and destiny.

Jesus demonstrated this well while on earth. He was presence driven and purpose shaped. Your priority is to have an intimate relationship with God, and out of that comes your life's accomplishments. Jesus revealed this in John 17:3-4, in the conversation He had with His Father a short time before He was arrested and taken into custody by Roman soldiers. He said, "And this is eternal life, that they may know You, the only true God, and Jesus Christ whom You have sent. I have glorified You on the earth. I have finished the work which You have given Me to do" (NKJV). When Jesus said, "this is eternal life," the statement that follows is very important. He said that eternal life is knowing God.

There are two words in the verse, translated from the Greek language, that provide further understanding. The word *life* is *zoe*, and it means "the quality of life that is possessed by the one who gives it." Jesus is offering to everyone the same quality of life He enjoys with the heavenly Father, which includes the same love, closeness, acceptance, anointing, authority, and so forth. He referenced this same word, *life,* earlier in John 10:10: "I have come that they may have life, and that they may have it more abundantly" (NKJV). Jesus is making the same quality of life He has available to you in abundance.

# *Jesus is offering to everyone the same quality of life He enjoys with the heavenly Father.*

Jesus gives generously and without limitations. An example of this is the statement He made in John 7:37-38, that if we come to Him and drink, out of our heart would flow rivers of living water. This a multiplication—you drink in His presence, and He multiples it into rivers of living water flowing out of you.

Hearing from Him positions you to live the life He intends. Paul says in Galatians 5:25, "If we live in the Spirit, let us also walk in the Spirit" (KJV). The word *live* is a verb that comes from the word *zoe.*

The word *walk* means "to line up or proceed in a row." You can believe you have the life of God in you and have already become what God wants you to be. All you need to do is cooperate with God's power already resident in you and activate it by simple faith or belief.

The second word from John 17:3 to understand is the word *know*. This word means "experience." God is all about relationships! The Bible can be summarized in the following sentence: The Father wants a family, Jesus wants a bride, the Holy Spirit wants a temple, or a person. God uses terms like *family, children, heirs, brother, friend,* and so forth throughout the Word. Another way to summarize God's intention is to say that He loves you into a place of abundant life where you are fully experiencing His love; then He wants you to give it away.

*Love* means to value, hold in high regard, and consider precious. You are designed by God to feel and experience His love for you! As a result of doing so, your self-worth and identity are transformed. When you experience His love, it impacts your trust in God. In a love environment, faith works. Therefore, the more you experience His love, the more faith—belief and trust—you can walk in.

# *Purpose is a proportionate mixture of what you do and how you do it.*

Another benefit of experiencing God's love is being able to love others. God's love teaches you how to treat others in a manner key to your ability to walk out your purpose. Purpose is a proportionate mixture of what you do and how you do it. Purpose demonstrated in the context of character and love produces a reputation that Proverbs 22:1 describes as better than "great riches" (ESV).

I have experienced challenging circumstances with people doing and saying hurtful things while I was actively flowing in my purpose. I'm sure you can relate to having emotions rising up and all sorts of thoughts swirling about. When you lean in to the trust you have developed, you can grab hold of those emotions before you say or do something you may regret. In the moment, you might want to defend yourself or even give someone a piece of your mind. But if you pause and talk with God at His throne of grace, you'll find mercy and grace to love, honor, and bless that person.

You can receive love from God freely and without limitation, and it's not something you need to manufacture. Romans 5:5 says that God's love is poured into our hearts by the Holy Spirit. And Jesus said that love is the number-one way His followers will be recognized. First Corinthians 13 goes so far as saying that without love, everything else is meaningless.

In John 17:4, Jesus completes His thoughts about experiencing God. He said, "I glorified you on earth, having accomplished the work that you gave me to do" (ESV). You operate out of a relationship with God, and your life, activities, and work are reflections of God. You bring Him glory in the way you conduct yourself and by accomplishing what He gives you to do. Actively experiencing God and being shaped by Him are the keys to being able to withstand turbulence in your life. Jesus spoke about this in Luke 6:47-48: "Everyone who comes to me and hears my words and does them, I will show you what he is like: he is like a man building a house, who dug deep and laid the foundation on the rock. And when a flood arose, the stream broke against that house and could not shake it, because it had been well built" (ESV).

## *Your life is well built and structured upon God's strength and not your own works.*

There is a heavenly blueprint for your life, and in your experience with Jesus you can hear His words and understand what your purpose is and how to walk it out. In life, you may experience overwhelming circumstances, forcefully attempting to bring destruction to your life and purpose, but according to God's Word you cannot be shaken. Your life is well built and structured upon God's strength and not your own works.

In verse 49, those who experience God but don't act upon His words subject themselves to a life susceptible to disappointment and even destruction. "But the one who hears and does not do them is like a man who built a house on the ground without a foundation. When the stream broke against it, immediately it fell, and the ruin of that house was great" (Luke 6:49, ESV).

Your relationship is a love journey—a lifetime of discovery—where you come to know who God is, who you are, and how to accomplish what He wants you to achieve. I promise you, His plan for your life is better than anything you could imagine on your own, so get prepared to dream big with God.

## ACTIVATION

Think about the quality of life Jesus wants you to experience. Write down your thoughts and the emotions you feel about having the same love, closeness, acceptance, anointing, and authority Jesus has.

Think about how you would like your life to look as it pertains to your experience with God. Write down what that quality of life looks like in the various areas of your life—personal, family, community, workplace, and so forth.

Think back on a particular experience when you trusted God and pursued His will in your life. Express gratitude for His faithfulness during turbulent times of resistance.

### Heart-to-Heart Series:

https://www.youtube.com/
playlist?list=PLuh1d30Agdvh4WE6C7jn5GkDYgJY1gVod

You are an Esther or a Paul and God has an amazing call on your life.

# Chapter Three

# Purpose Lived Out in Scripture

I loved visiting my Grandma Juliar when I was growing up. She lived on a farm, and I would stay with her often, all the way into my high school years. She always had some project she was working on, like sewing clothes, canning food, or piecing together a quilt. As a matter of fact, for the first several years of my life, most of my clothes were made by my grandma. I remember how exciting it was to drive with Grandma to the fabric store to pick out a pattern and material. When we arrived back home, she would carefully take the pattern out, trim it, and methodically pin it to the fabric, then cut out all the pieces. Within a matter of hours, I would have a new dress made from the very fabric I picked out!

I always wanted to help, but mainly I would watch, as I was too young to handle the sharp scissors and too small to reach the sewing machine pedal. However, as I got a little older, I started sewing my own clothes. I didn't attend formal classes to learn how to sew, but I learned from watching my grandma. I learned by example, which continues to be the most effective way for me to learn. During the time when I began seeking God about purpose and destiny—to really get it and apply it—I knew I would need examples to follow and learn from.

We're going to dive deep into the experience of two individuals, Esther and Jesus, and discover how they accomplished their God-given purpose in life. I think you would agree these two are great biblical examples to learn from. One of the things that stood out to me was how they both walked in harmony with God and trusted Him. Trust is an essential ingredient in your walk with God and the resulting success you achieve. Trust was hard for me. I felt my trust had been shattered so many times that I didn't know what it looked like to truly trust God. It would have been like trying to sew an outfit without the benefit of observing and learning from my grandma.

*The deeper your relationship goes with God, the greater your trust in Him grows.*

You can face challenges as a victorious overcomer rather than a victim when your confidence is in God, His consistency, His love, and His generosity toward you. The deeper your relationship goes with God, the greater your trust in Him grows, knowing He'll provide for you in every situation. You are building a personal history with God based upon trust in who He is and what He has already promised to do.

Esther was one of the first examples (and my favorite) I grabbed on to of someone who discovered and lived out her purpose. The book of Esther reveals how God prepared Esther for a special purpose, "for such a time as this" (4:14, ESV), and orchestrated all of the intricate events and details to rescue and save His covenant people from the destruction planned for them. Esther was a Jew, living among the exiles in Persia (modern-day Iran) in approximately 480 B.C. Her mother and father had passed away, and she found herself in the home of her uncle Mordecai as a young, single woman. God knew her purpose was to become queen of the empire and rescuer of the Jews. But Esther hadn't begun her life knowing what she was called to do. Throughout the story, you can see how God had His hand of direction on her, working on her behalf.

There was an evil man named Haman, an official of King Ahasuerus, who, as a result of his jealousy and hate, sought to eradicate the Jewish people. The book does not mention God's name, although His fingerprints are clearly visible in every passage. The story documents the origins of the Jewish observance of Purim, a celebration of Israel's survival and God's faithfulness. God's sovereign hand preserved His people, utilizing Esther's purpose. God saw the outcome and worked with Esther and Mordecai and those around them to bring it to pass. You may not fully understand the powerful impact of your life upon the future, but you'll be celebrated for your faithfulness to live your purpose for God's glory. Let's take a closer look at some of the details surrounding Esther's incredible life.

King Ahasuerus wanted beautiful, young virgins added to his harem with the intention of eventually choosing one of the concubines to be his queen. His officers went throughout the kingdom, which was comprised of 127 provinces from as far away as India and Ethiopia, and took young girls back to the king's palace to be presented as prospects. Can you imagine how frightening it would have been for young girls to be forcibly removed from their homes and families and sent to a foreign city?

Esther was one of those girls taken from her home, but in line with the call on her life, she received favor over all the others from the king's eunuch. It didn't stop there. She kept winning favor in the eyes of all who saw her. Operating in your purpose—in alignment with God's design—brings favor. Functionally speaking, favor is the attraction and protection of God upon an individual, which causes people, circumstances, and powers to align and cooperate with you. Proverbs 8:35 tells us, "For he who finds me finds life and obtains favor from the Lord" (NASB95). Finding yourself in your purpose is life giving, and God's favor joins you for success.

Esther experienced God's favor in the midst of a difficult situation that required risking her life to speak out on behalf of her people. What a heavy load for a young girl to bear! Esther was in the palace, facing a huge challenge. She had to determine if she was willing to potentially give her life for her people. Was it the right thing for her to do? What was the plan and the timing? Purpose is often revealed in an idea of what to do (vision), and then other factors come into play, such as methodology (how), timing (when), and collaboration with others.

In Esther's case, she received some advice from Mordecai: "For if you remain completely silent at this time, relief and deliverance will arise for the Jews from another place, but you and your father's house will perish. Yet who knows whether you have come to the kingdom for such a time as this?" (4:14, NKJV).

Esther then made her decision and responded to Mordecai, "Go, gather all the Jews to be found in Susa, and hold a fast on my behalf, and do not eat or drink for three days, night or day. I and my young women will also fast as you do. Then I will go to the king, though it is against the law, and if I perish, I perish" (4:16, ESV).

When Esther asked her maids to fast, I have wondered if she was asking them to fast for her challenge with the decision to go before the king unannounced or for the outcome. Esther had everything in the world at the time. She had attained royalty, all the maids and servants one could ask for, and she could do or have anything she desired. The world would say that she has attained the perfect life. Why then would she risk her life for people she didn't personally know? I believe she had to seriously consider her actions.

*Whether you have attained success or notoriety in the world or not, I believe eventually you have to decide if you're going to pursue the things of the world or God's purpose.*

Notice that verse 14 says, "who knows whether you have attained royalty for such a time as this [and for this very purpose]?" (AMP). Then, at the end of verse 16, Esther declared, "Then I will go to the king…and if I perish, I perish." Whether you have attained success or notoriety in the world or not, I believe eventually you have to decide if you're going to pursue the things of the world or God's purpose. Often, even though we may not be faced with potential death as Esther was, we are faced with a decision of giving up the things of the world to pursue God's purpose. The beautiful aspect I love about Esther's story is not only did she save her people, but she went on to affect God's kingdom for years to come. Esther made the decision to follow God. In that decision, though she risked much, God was faithful to take her to a higher place than she could've ever attained on her own.

Esther is an inspiring example of someone willing to be used by God to bring about His desired outcome. She received His favor and ability to accomplish her divine task. Willingness is a key factor in stepping into your purpose. You are designed in the image of God, and He specifically created you with a free will. He has a plan and a purpose for your life. However, your free will and your choice to participate is an active ingredient to your success.

Can you imagine if Mary, the mother of Jesus, had turned down the angel Gabriel's offer to bring Jesus into the world? She could have told him her dream was to get married to Joseph, her fiancé, and she didn't want a scandal. Mary activated her purpose with her willingness to follow God's direction and obedience to see it through.

Let's now turn to the life of Jesus for another example of living out purpose. There's so much we can learn from how Jesus lived His life on earth. We'll look closely and see how He operated, examine His relationship with the Father, and measure the impact He had on the people around Him. Jesus is the perfect model for us. And remember, He offers you the same quality and abundance of life that He possesses. This abundant life is also known as *zoe* life.

In Revelation 13:8, the Word says that before the earth was formed, Jesus looked ahead and planned to die as the perfect sacrifice for mankind, His treasured creation. The apostle John said this about Jesus' purpose: "For this purpose the Son of God was manifested, that He might destroy the works of the devil" (1 John 3:8, NKJV).

What are the main works of the devil? They are sin, sickness, demonic torment, poverty, destruction, deception, and fear. Jesus became the solution by providing salvation for sin, healing for sickness, freedom from the demonic, truth to set people free of lies, abundant life, and genuine love, which removes fear and judgment. The problem Jesus came to solve started in the Garden of Eden. Adam and Eve chose disobedience and lost their connection with God and their ability to see life through His eyes. This happened because they were deceived by the devil and believed a lie about God. They believed God was not good and had not created them in His image. They didn't see God as their source and thought they could become like Him. Instead, they wanted to be their own source and have the ability to choose between good and evil.

This idea is at the root of all sin and unbelief. If people decide what is good and evil independent of what God says in His Word and in relationship with Him, they'll set themselves on a course of destruction. In Joshua 24:15, God admonished the people to "choose this day whom you will serve" (ESV). The word *choose* in Hebrew is the image of plotting a ship's course. Moving into your purpose and destiny begins with your choice to "plot your course" toward the destination God has and to cooperate with His direction and development in your life.

# *Jesus faced challenges while living out His purpose and learned to choose God's view and opinion over His own.*

Jesus came to reconnect people to their loving, heavenly Father and enable them to see through His eyes. When Jesus said in Luke 4:18 that He came to give sight to the blind, He was primarily speaking of spiritual blindness. God wants you to know Him and to see, understand, and experience His reality.

Jesus mentioned another aspect of His purpose in John 10:10. He said, "The thief comes only to steal and kill and destroy. I came that they may have life and have it abundantly" (ESV). This is the same life (*zoe*) that I discussed earlier.

Jesus faced challenges while living out His purpose and learned to choose God's view and opinion over His own. To do that, He exalted the eyes of His heart over His natural view. That strategy provided the capability to access unlimited resources to meet every need, and you have that same capability. An example of this is in Mark 6:41, where He took five loaves of bread and two fish and fed the multitude of people. The verse says, "he looked up to heaven and said a blessing and broke the loaves" (ESV). In the original language, it reads, "He looked into heaven and recovered His sight." That phrase, *recovered sight,* is the same as in Luke 4:18, "recovering of sight to the blind" (ESV). Jesus saw the need in the natural and understood His limitation, so He looked to the Father. He recovered His ability to see the unlimited resources of the kingdom of heaven, then activated the miracle of multiplying food. Jesus teaches us to take the limits off our situation and see the opportunities and resources available to fulfill our purpose.

Jesus learned to activate grace for empowerment and timing in walking out His purpose. In John 7 when the Jews tried to kill Him, He said it was not yet His time. In the garden of Gethsemane, as He talked with the Father, He was not trying to avoid the cross. I believe He wanted to confirm it was the will of His Father to go to the cross at that time. Once He confirmed the timing, He wanted to receive the strength to move forward with their plan.

Jesus was fully man and fully God, and without His Father's empowerment, the cross would have been impossible to face. Hebrews 2:9 says that Jesus tasted death for every man by the grace of God. It was in His communication with the Father that He received the grace to face the cross, become sin, and endure the devastating separation. In becoming sin, He took on the curse of the law according to Galatians 3:13. Grace is God's ability working in you, making it possible to do what you can't do in your own strength or ability.

There are many more examples of Jesus living His purpose that you can learn and grow from. I will end this chapter with an example that impacts all of us as God's sons and daughters. Jesus came to reveal the Father and to show people what God was really like. He said that if people knew Him, they would have known the Father (John 8:19). Later, in John 20:21, Jesus commissioned His disciples with the same tasks the Father had given Him. In the same way the Father had sent Him, Jesus was sending them.

We have the privilege and honor to reveal our heavenly Father to the world and be problem solvers who influence society. The way to do that is to live out our God-given purpose.

## ACTIVATION

Journal how you feel about being born "for such a time as this."

What would "recover sight to the blind" mean to you in your everyday decisions and circumstances?

Write down a few thoughts on how you see God using you as a problem solver and person of influence.

Stories about purpose are throughout the Bible, whether it's Noah building an ark or Joseph providing for Israel during a famine. Find stories about purpose. Identify the key elements of the story, snag the takeaways, and write them down to learn from God's wisdom.

Chapter Four

# Fear Not, on Purpose

In 2010, we lived in Minnetonka, Minnesota, and life was good. I had climbed the corporate ladder and ran several divisions at the executive level for a billion-dollar bank. My husband, Tim, and I had built our dream house, and my son was in a great school and had wonderful friends. We were living the life we had planned.

On the day it all changed, I kissed my husband and left for work like every other day. I was working in my office when our Human Resources Manager, Marnie, came in and said, "Karen, something has happened with Tim. The hospital has been trying to contact you."

"Oh, what's going on with Tim?" I asked. I thought she was referring to the interim bank president, who was visiting our site.

Marnie replied, "No, your husband, Tim. You need to call Hennepin County Medical Center."

*Oh, my goodness, what did he do?* I figured he probably injured himself while at his construction worksite. I called the Hennepin County Medical Center number she gave me and found I was speaking with the coroner. My husband had died at 8:00 that morning

There is a battlefield
in our mind
between the Word
of God and fear.
Which will you
agree with?

after dropping off my son at basketball camp. We had absolutely no warning and found ourselves thrown into a chaos I can't even begin to describe.

We later learned the details of that day, but through the shock I could not process anything the coroner tried to explain over the phone. After Tim dropped off Levi at the gym where he helped coach inner city kids, Tim witnessed a car accident. He pulled over and called 911 to report the accident. The operator requested that he wait for the officer's arrival to give his report. Tim agreed but didn't say anything else, and the operator assumed he had fallen asleep. When the officer arrived and knocked on Tim's passenger side window, he found Tim dead behind the steering wheel.

Fourteen years earlier, Tim had undergone open-heart surgery to replace a valve in his heart. Since then, he had been healthy and strong and had passed a thorough exam every year, including one just two weeks prior. On this day, Tim's heart had simply stopped. The coroner told us he had no pain, but just that fast he was gone. I couldn't comprehend how this had happened. Where was God in all of this, and what was I going to do now?

Let me tell you, that was a defining moment in my life. I had to figure out how to raise my son without his father, who was also Levi's absolute best friend. My protector, companion, and partner in life was gone, and I was utterly overwhelmed. The days and months following were difficult. As a matter of fact, there were days I couldn't keep any food down. We attended a strong church and had an incredible support system at Levi's school, for which we were grateful. I knew God had not taken my husband, but I felt far from being a strong woman of faith.

I was already struggling with fear of failure and rejection, and now this. Honestly, I didn't know what I was going to do, and I became consumed with fear. I knew fear had to go, but the question was how? Everything I had tried up to this point was not working, and that was the issue. Dealing with fear is one of those areas I thought I had to take on in my own strength. I believed that it was my duty to muster up enough faith to drive out fear, because the Bible instructs us multiple times to "Fear not." But I learned that I had way too much coming at me to be able to successfully fight that battle on my own.

*Fear is a tactic of the enemy meant to stop us from fulfilling God's purpose in our lives.*

I had come to the end of myself. So often, that's the place where things have started to turn the corner for me. The Bible tells us fearful thoughts are tormenting, and I certainly understood the reality of that statement. Fear is a tactic of the enemy meant to stop us from fulfilling God's purpose in our lives, and it had to go. But how? I was looking for the right formula or steps to fix this fear problem. But I was looking for the wrong thing. Instead of looking for what I could do, I needed to look at Jesus and His Word to receive what He had already made available for me.

The first step and foundation for living a life free of fear is found in 1 John 4:18, which reads, "There is no fear in love [dread does not exist]. But perfect (complete, full-grown) love drives out fear, because fear involves [the expectation of divine] punishment, so the one who is afraid [of God's judgment] is not perfected in love [has not grown into a sufficient understanding of God's love]" (AMP). The bottom line was that I needed to gain a strong understanding of God's love for me. Everything springboards from there. Could this be the key to overcome fear of failure, fear of rejection, and more? The answer is a resounding "Yes!" With an understanding of God's unconditional love for me, I was able to exalt the Word of God over my thoughts, fears, imaginations, and eventually the behaviors I had developed.

As I dug into the Word to find out what God said about fear, I came to understand there are two different kinds. Interestingly, there are commands both to fear *not* and to fear *God*. So which is correct, and is there a contradiction? They are actually both correct because they have different root meanings.

Let's look at the difference between these two to clear up any confusion. Proverbs 28:14 says that "Blessed is the one who fears the Lord always, but whoever hardens his heart will fall into calamity" (ESV). Here you have a warning to fear God. But in the next chapter of Proverbs, we read: "The fear of man lays a snare, but whoever trusts in the Lord is safe" (29:25, ESV). Which is right? They both are! Stay with me here.

Fearing the Lord doesn't mean to be afraid of Him. Not at all. We have all grown up with our own concept of the fear of God. If you are like me, it was not a positive one. It was the thought that God may become upset and "bonk" me over the head when I made a mistake or did something wrong. Studies show that a person's greatest fear is that of the unknown. It makes sense that if we're not quite sure of God's character or His love for us, it would open the door for fear to have a place in our life. That was certainly the case for me.

The fear of the Lord is not a negative concept or reason for concern; it is just misunderstood. The Old Testament describes the covenant nature of God, and here God tells people not to fear. Jesus appeared to His disciples after His resurrection and told them not to fear. God does not want you to have fear in your heart. He does want you to have a personal relationship with Him and trust His Word, knowing you are loved and accepted. Perfect love "casts out" or displaces fear (1 John 4:18), which means love and fear cannot live together.

When you open yourself to the truth about God, you experience His reassuring love, which removes fear. You may wonder why the Old Testament, as specifically worded in the King James Version, tells us to "Fear not," while other verses promote the idea of fearing God. Fear yes, or fear no? As we study this closer, we learn that the biblical concept of the fear of God is more of a concern that our actions may hurt God's heart, just as we don't want to hurt or disappoint our parents, spouse, and other loved ones. It's the idea that we love God and consider Him precious; we value our relationship with Him, and we would not want our actions to hurt Him.

# God wants you to relate to Him out of love, not fear. His thoughts of you are loving, positive, and kind.

God is love, and as your loving Father He will not break your heart or bring harm to you in any way. He will never give up on you, and He wants the best for you in every area of your life. He does not place demands on you. Rather, He wants you to relate to Him out of love, not fear. His thoughts of you are loving, positive, and kind, and He will never abandon or let you down. In response, you make the choice to love Him and not hurt Him. You're only human, and at times you may make mistakes and become distant, but God is quick to restore relationship with you.

Jesus, who came to reveal the Father, gave a very clear explanation regarding the fear of the Lord. When Jesus was in the desert and tempted by the devil, He quoted an Old Testament Scripture: "Then Jesus said to him, 'Be gone, Satan! For it is written, "You shall worship the Lord your God and him only shall you serve"''" (Matt. 4:10, ESV). Jesus was quoting Deuteronomy 6:13, which says, "It is the Lord your God you shall fear. Him you shall serve and by his name you shall swear" (ESV). Jesus changed the word *fear* to worship. The word *fear* in the Old Testament carries the idea of awe, respect, and love that results in worship. God wants us to have an awe of Him that results in worship, not fear.

Now, let's contrast this healthy fear or awe with the unhealthy fear the Lord commands us not to have. The latter brings worry, anxiety, and keeps you up at night, imagining things that haven't yet happened—and may never happen—in your life. The following verse is one that has helped me in this area: "We destroy arguments and every lofty opinion raised against the knowledge of God, and take every thought captive to obey Christ" (2 Cor. 10:5, ESV). I used to think I needed to grab myself by the collar and bring my thoughts into the obedience of Christ, feeling as though I was in trouble with the principal. But God gave me a revelation one day as I was reading this verse. I realized that He isn't scolding me, but He's loving me and telling me to cast down that fearful thought because it's crowding the knowledge of God out of my mind and heart.

Take the example of being afraid while raising your children. God is saying that every time you have a fearful thought about your child, reject it. Next, bring every thought into captivity to the obedience of Christ. I used to think I needed to carry condemnation for my thoughts and do a "penance" to be free. But now I know that when I bring my fearful thoughts into the obedience of Christ and exalt what He says in His Word about my child as truth—my child is blessed, full of peace, and obedient to the Lord—over the fearful thoughts, He brings peace to my situation.

*One of the most common hindrances to your destiny is the fear of man.*

Another example of unhealthy fear, and one of the most common hindrances to your destiny, is the fear of man. This simply means that you care too much about what other people think of you. You identify more with others' opinions than God's opinion, and it causes you to worry about how you're perceived by other people. In some cases, the fear of man can cause you to step outside of your purpose and destiny in God just to please others. This is an indication that you're not trusting Him to bring promotion or right connections. Instead, you're putting your trust in people to do what only God can do.

In Isaiah 51:7, God is reminding us of who we are: "Listen to Me, you who know righteousness, you people in whose heart is My law: do not fear the reproach of men, nor be afraid of their insults" (NKJV). He is telling us to "fear not the reproach of men" because He knew we would deal with the opinions of men.

One thing you can be sure of as you travel through life is that not everyone will like you. As you courageously step into your purpose and destiny, there will be resistance. Often, the enemy tries to get us to retaliate and function on his level as accuser of the brethren. No matter whom an accusation is coming through, the enemy is behind accusing the brethren, and he does it to make us fear men.

The Bible says you have favor and good understanding in the sight of God and man (see Prov. 3:4). You can stand on that promise. Of course, you care about and love people and don't want to be hard or crass toward anyone but always exude the love of God. But be aware, if God has a call on your life and He has given you an assignment to complete, you will be criticized.

My friend Andrew Wommack tells a story where the Lord showed him running a race, and someone heckled him from the crowd. Andrew left the track and went into the stands to argue with the heckler. The Lord said, "If you're going to run your race, you can't be distracted. You must stay on the track." We are all in a race to complete our destiny, and we must stay focused on our own race. You should be kind to others, but stay undistracted.

*Fear is thinking about something that could happen but isn't actually happening and may never happen.*

Fear is defeated in the mind. Fear is thinking about something that could happen but isn't actually happening and may never happen. If you logically examine what is causing you fear, worry, and anxiety, it's almost a 100 percent guarantee that it is based in your mind. This means that between your ears, you have created a world based in non-reality. My friend Elizabeth describes it as playing a movie in our mind. It's a ploy of the enemy to get you to believe a lie and stop you from getting where you need to go. This is not something to be condemned about but to learn from, so you can take the Word of God as truth and trust Him completely.

Developing a process to filter your thoughts begins with identifying a lie and understanding the source of fear and lies. John 10:10 tells us,

FEAR NOT, ON PURPOSE

"The thief comes only in order to steal and kill and destroy. I came that they may have and enjoy life, and have it in abundance [to the full, till it overflows]" (AMP). Which camp are your thoughts in? There is one camp that will eventually steal, kill, or destroy you, which is the enemy's camp. Then there is the camp of "life more abundant," which is Jesus' camp. The enemy has no truth in him, so thoughts from him can only be lies. Jesus is the Prince of Peace, so thoughts from Him can only bring peace.

If you feel anxious, worried, and stressed, you're entertaining thoughts from the enemy, and all he can do is lie. Jesus said it like this: "Ye are of your father the devil, and the lusts of your father ye will do. He was a murderer from the beginning, and abode not in the truth, because there is no truth in him. When he speaketh a lie, he speaketh of his own: for he is a liar, and the father of it" (John 8:44, KJV). I have learned to connect any fear-filled thought to a lie from the enemy. Once I do that, I reject the lie and speak out the truth, which is God's Word, regarding the situation. "God has not given us a spirit of fear, but of power and of love and of a sound mind" (2 Tim. 1:7, NKJV). Once the thought is identified as a lie, you can apply 2 Corinthians 10:5. Take that thought captive, and replace it with truth. This is literally how I learned to process thoughts because I am so logical. I need to see it in the Word then know how to apply it. Simply put:

Fear is from the enemy.

There is no truth in the enemy.

Therefore, there is no truth in fear.

Does this thought bring fear?

55

If so, it is not from the Lord.

Exchange that thought for a promise in God's Word.

Agree with the Word, and turn away from fear.

What you agree with is what has power in your life.

We have so many precious promises to hold on to. In our world today, there's a vast amount of conflicting information, causing thoughts of fear, worry, uncertainty, and anxiety. Remember, God is good and brings peace. The enemy is bad and brings fear. God knew we would struggle with fear, so He gave us a way out. He addresses fear and puts it under our feet over and over throughout His Word. He did that for us. Fear is not only able to be defeated, it is already defeated.

## ACTIVATION

Differentiate between the fear of God versus the fear of man.

Can you identify your chain of reasoning?

When you recognize a fearful thought, what do you currently do with it, and what does the Word say to do with it?

Take a week and practice this process with your thoughts. Keep a journal, and watch how the Lord works.

Fear is from the enemy.

There is no truth in the enemy.

Therefore, there is no truth in fear.

Does this thought bring fear?

If so, it is not from the Lord.

Exchange that thought for a promise in God's Word.

Agree with the Word, and turn away from fear.

What you agree with is what has power in your life.

## Fear Not Download:

https://drive.google.com/file/d/1tJ6jIClABFIiwkAmE8XiO_SE4wb5eB5H/view?usp=sharing

## Success Made Simple:

https://www.youtube.com/playlist?list=PLuh1d30Agdvj_qGqHcAk_HvtFXSxSiBg8

# Do you see yourself past, present and future the way God sees you?

# Chapter Five

# Glass Ceilings Shattered on Purpose

A glass ceiling is an invisible hindrance that you're not fully aware of, intended to limit your success. A glass ceiling is another tool the enemy uses to distract or derail you from fulfilling your purpose. Limitations can be placed on you from the outside, but more often they come from the inside. Much of what affects your life begins in your mind, like fear. Daily learning to see yourself as God sees you and remembering the value He places on you will give you the courage to push through any glass ceiling you face. He sent Jesus to pay your ransom, wash you clean as new fallen snow, and open up endless opportunities to you.

Life is full of experiences—some good and some bad—which mold your future. There are times you may carry those past experiences into new parts of your life. Good experiences can bring joy, hope, and life with them, but bad experiences bring fear, pain, and lies. The latter can impose limits that you unconsciously submit to. Sometimes you're actually believing lies that could drive your life in a direction you don't want to go.

It had been nine years since I unexpectedly became a widow, and it was seven years since my son, Levi, and I moved to Colorado for him to attend Bible college. After that, I stayed in Colorado to work at Andrew Wommack Ministries and grow my real estate business. During that time, I had many conversations with the Lord about the possibility of getting married again. I had an agreement with God: I would pursue His purpose in my life, and He would take care of bringing me a husband. The agreement was working fine at the beginning, but in the entire seven years I lived in Colorado, I did not have one official date. It was looking a bit bleak in the husband department. People told me my husband was on the way, so I was looking, but no one materialized.

As I was going about my business at the ministry, Lance Wallnau came in to record some programs in October 2017. He had brought a good friend with him, named David Metcalfe, along with one of his team members. We had to solidify details of the programs, so we all met for dinner. Levi had connected with Lance prior to this trip, so he agreed to come with me that evening, which was highly unusual. Lance introduced his friend Dave to me, and Dave ended up sitting across the table from me, next to Levi. As we talked business, Dave and Levi carried on a conversation about trees, as Levi is an arborist and really enjoys talking about trees.

I had assumed Dave was married and didn't give it another thought. But little did I know that during the dinner, Lance and his team member were texting each other, asking, "What do you think about Dave and Karen?" In May 2018, seven months after that dinner, I received a call from Lance's wife, Annabelle, asking me if I would be open to Dave calling me. I agreed, knowing that if Lance and Annabelle were behind the match-making, I needed to pay attention.

Interestingly, during the time between when I first met Dave and him calling me, two different men had reached out to see if I would be interested in going to dinner, but neither followed up after the initial connection. I was starting to wonder if God needed a little help, but the story of Abram and Sarai trying to fulfill God's promise themselves was enough to keep me in my lane. As Dave and I began getting to know each other through phone conversations and a few visits, to say I was wavering would be a major understatement. I didn't make it easy for Dave at all. I was hesitant to move forward in a relationship, but I couldn't logically explain why. Thinking back on that time, I am so grateful to both Dave and the Lord for not quitting on me.

*No matter where limitations come from, God is the One who removes them.*

During the fall of that year, an opportunity opened for me to attend an executive retreat at Bethel Church in Redding, California. During the retreat, attendees were scheduled for something called a *sozo*. I had tried to back out, but it was highly encouraged, so I went. Little did I know I would discover a "glass ceiling" in my life. At Bethel, sozo is a ministry that helps people get to the root of anything hindering their inner health or walking out their purpose. It's not a counseling session but a time of interacting with Father, Son, and Holy Spirit for freedom and wholeness in order to pursue your destiny.

During the session, I was asked to share two areas in my life where I needed clarity, and we would talk and pray about those for direction. I shared about this man named Dave I had met and how I wasn't sure if he was someone God wanted me to be with. As the facilitator asked me questions, we began to seek the Lord. God revealed a strong wall of self-protection I had built around myself that kept me from being able to see what God was doing in my life concerning Dave. We prayed to break down the wall, and from that day forward I knew that God had brought Dave into my life to be my husband. I had been unaware of a glass ceiling in the area of intimacy and relationships built from years of hurt and disappointment. As I look at Dave today and reflect on the beauty of our marriage, I can hardly believe I almost walked away from such an amazing husband, who is part of my God-given destiny.

No matter where limitations come from, God is the One who removes them: "Out of my deep anguish and pain I prayed, and God, you helped me as a father. You came to my rescue and broke open the way into a beautiful and broad place. Now I know, Lord, that you are for me, and I will never fear what man can do to me. For you stand beside me as my hero who rescues me. I've seen with my own eyes the defeat of my enemies. I've triumphed over them all! Lord, it is so much better to trust in you to save me than to put my confidence in someone else" (Ps. 118:5-8, TPT). He rescues you and fights for you as a father and a hero. He is on your side and wants the best for you.

When you recognize limitations and where they come from, you can begin breaking through your glass ceiling. If a limitation is holding you back, exalt the Word of God and what He says about you. Take the process outlined in Chapter 4 for fear, and apply it to each of the areas of limitation you identify in your life. Let's look at some categories that most limitations fit into.

## PAST EXPERIENCES

Those of you who have gone through difficult and traumatic times or made mistakes, you know the past can deter you from receiving God's best; it can limit or hold you back. If you've had a bad experience in a relationship, such as a marriage ending, your temptation can be to apply your past experience of failure to your current situation in life and enter the new relationship with a bias God doesn't want you to have. It could be the same thing in business. A bankruptcy or a failure in business can limit you when God puts on your heart to start a new business. If you have not dealt with the past and renewed your mind to the Word of God, you can take the expectation of failure into your new business.

*Be encouraged. You're not destined to repeat the same mistakes or failures over and over in your life.*

Isaiah 43:16-19 says, "Thus says the Lord, who makes a way in the sea, a path in the mighty waters, who brings forth chariot and horse, army and warrior; they lie down, they cannot rise, they are extinguished, quenched like a wick: 'Remember not the former things, nor consider the things of old. Behold, I am doing a new thing; now it springs forth, do you not perceive it? I will make a way in the wilderness and rivers in the desert'" (ESV).

In this passage, the Lord was speaking to Israel. God was encouraging Israel that He won't hold their past against them. But Israel had some very difficult past experiences. Think about the difficult past experiences of your life. When you look at this Scripture, the Lord is reminding you that He has created the sea. He has created the waters. He has even created the chariot and the horse, the army and the mighty warrior. He is telling you, "I am God, and I have created everything."

Then He says to forget the past, and He encourages you that these things will not rise up again. He is extending an invitation to you to say, "You know what, God? You have created everything. You know my heart. You know my situation. I don't want to take these past failures or bad experiences into a new stage of life. I hear You telling me that my future life is not going to be like my past."

God says, "Do not remember the former things or ponder the things in the past. Listen carefully, I am about to do a new thing." He's doing a brand-new thing, not the old thing again. Be encouraged. You're not destined to repeat the same mistakes or failures over and over in your life. God has a plan to bring good even from your mistakes. Do you have something in your past that has created a mindset, a stronghold, or an expectation of falling short of God's best for you? Purposely grab hold of that and say, "I break those old thought patterns and believe God is going to do a new thing in my life in the name of Jesus." Find a Scripture with a promise that encourages your faith. You'll be able to thank God for all the things He has provided for you. Amen.

Psalm 45:10 reads, "Now listen, daughter, pay attention, and forget about your past" (TPT). Wow, that is awesome! But there's even more in verse 10: "Put behind you every attachment to the familiar, even those who once were close to you!" This is amazing because He is commanding you to forget about your past. The enemy loves to bring up your past, and he'll do it at times when you are tired, down on yourself, or confused. But God says to forget the past—He has forgotten it—and look to the future He has prepared for you.

Losing my first husband without any warning was traumatic. But if I had continued to relive that trauma in my mind, I wouldn't have been able to move forward with joy. Instead, I held on to Romans 8:28, "And we know [with great confidence] that God [who is deeply concerned about us] causes all things to work together [as a plan] for good for those who love God, to those who are called according to His plan and purpose" (AMP). God will transform those things that happened, that were meant to cause harm.

As you cooperate with Him, exalt Him, and love Him, you'll start to see the life He has for you in His Word. You don't need to relive past trauma. You can look at things the way God sees them, and the past becomes a distant memory used for your good. Today, I can look back on what happened and see how God has taken what the enemy meant for my harm and turned it for good in my life. I absolutely can. Praise Jesus.

---

## PAST SIN

Look at your past—no matter the situation—and determine whether you have dealt with it through the blood of Jesus. Maybe you never had a true revelation of what God has actually done in your life. Do you see past sin and allow it to limit you because you feel you're not worthy? I'm going to show you how to release it through the Word of God. This area sneaks up on people who don't realize they are still holding themselves to past sin. When you're able to release this, you'll have so much life open up to you. Let's get into the Word and see what God has to say about past sins.

*When you are born again, you have received everything in the spirit. Legally, everything is paid for, but you and I must actively respond and receive it.*

"Now, if anyone is enfolded into Christ, he has become an entirely new creation. All that is related to the old order has vanished. Behold, everything is fresh and new. And God has made all things new, and reconciled us to himself, and given us the ministry of reconciling others to God. In other words, it was through the Anointed One that

God was shepherding the world, not even keeping records of their transgressions, and he has entrusted to us the ministry of opening the door of reconciliation to God. We are ambassadors of the Anointed One who carry the message of Christ to the world, as though God were tenderly pleading with them directly through our lips. So we tenderly plead with you on Christ's behalf, 'Turn back to God and be reconciled to him.' For God made the only one who did not know sin to become sin for us, so that we who did not know righteousness might become the righteousness of God through our union with him" (2 Cor. 5:17-21, TPT).

You have become an entirely new creation. All that is related to the old order has vanished, and all things are made new. That is so powerful. Does it mean only some things are new? No, that's not what Paul said. He said everything is fresh and new, and you are enfolded in Christ. You are a new creature. Praise God, His cleansing is continual. When you are born again, you have received everything legally in the spirit. Legally, everything is paid for, but you and I must respond and receive it, which is a very active thing.

In 2010 shortly after Tim had passed away, I developed a lump in my breast. I was doing everything I knew to do, including reading, speaking, and believing God's Word. I knew what the Word said concerning my healing, but I didn't have that ligament, or the connection from the Word, to the manifestation in my body. I saw what Scripture said, but what was happening in the natural and what I was dealing with in my physical body was not matching up with the fact that I knew God had already provided healing for me. I was really struggling.

I went with some friends to a church service in Des Moines, Iowa, and I went up front for prayer after the service. The minister looked at me and said, "Tell me what's going on." I was in tears as I told him about the lump in my breast. He looked me straight in the eye and asked, "What lump? You don't have a lump." I didn't understand. I re-explained my problem to him, and he answered the same way: "What lump?" My first thought was, *I'm going to the bathroom to check and it will be gone,* which wasn't the case.

The minister spoke truth to me—what was true in the Spirit—and it caused me to understand what he meant when he asked, "What lump?" In the spirit I was completely healed, and in that moment it was enough for me to receive what God says about me. After that day, although it wasn't immediate, I forgot about it. I had received the truth in my mind and in my soul. I knew it was true, and when I actually thought about it again to check a few months later, it was completely gone. That's an example of actively receiving what God has already done. It requires humility to exalt what God says is true over how we feel or what our circumstances indicate.

God said, "Though your sins be as scarlet, they shall be as white as snow; though they be red like crimson, they shall be as wool" (Isa. 1:18, KJV). When you receive the finished work of Jesus and apply the blood of Jesus in your life, it remains. Nothing can remove it from you. It's something you have received, and God will never leave you or forsake you (see Heb. 13:5). There may be areas where you are limiting yourself because of past sins—areas where you have not fully received God's forgiveness. Jesus has the ability and willingness to forgive. If you are born again, when He and the Father look at you, they see you white as snow.

If God reveals that there's something from your past that you still hold yourself captive to or punish yourself for, know that He sees you spotlessly clean. It's important to receive this. God loves you so much that He said, "I have wiped them out for my own sake and I will not remember your sins" (Isa. 43:25, paraphrase). He'll remove your sins as far as the East is from the West (see Ps. 103:12). He blots them out. He throws them into the ocean for His own sake. If you're having trouble receiving forgiveness, sometimes you need to make a shift in how you feel about your sin. If you can't forget your past sins or mistakes for your own sake, do it for His sake. He's serious when He says He won't remember your sins. If He doesn't remember them, why do you?

I don't know anyone who has lived a perfect life, except Jesus. I don't know anyone who doesn't need the grace of God or to lean into what Jesus did. Coming to grips with the fact that Jesus already paid the price for peace, healing, success, hope, life, and so much more means that I don't need to punish myself for my sin or mistakes. When you learn to exalt the finished work of the blood of Jesus above past sins, the glass ceiling can no longer hold you back.

## BELIEVING LIES

Let me ask you this: What lies are you believing today? What have you allowed to take root in your mind that causes you to agree with the enemy instead of the truth of the Word? When you know the truth, you understand that the Father and the Son agreed that what

Jesus did was enough. This doesn't mean you're going to automatically receive the blessings of God because you and I have a free will. You will need to agree with and exalt the Word of God. If you agree with something negative in your life instead of the truth, you are the deciding factor. Your life will go in the direction of the lie you believe. You need to recognize that those things outside of God's will are lies, and then find the truth of what God says about those things instead. You can choose to take your mind, will, and emotions and line them up with the truth. This is a key to receiving God's best in your life and removing that glass ceiling.

*When you're in a fearful situation, you need people around who are able to speak truth to you.*

I had a situation some weeks ago when I was really tired. I was going on three hours of sleep a night, and I've learned that those are the times I have to really guard my mind. When I'm tired, I don't always have the mental strength to capture thoughts or realize I am being sucked into deception. It was a situation involving a phone call, and I had worked up a "scene" in my mind.

I shared the situation with my husband, Dave, and went down the list of things I had assumed were happening. He looked at me and said, "First of all, let's talk about the truth of the situation." He stopped me in my tracks and used the process I am describing here. He started speaking about the truth of the situation and what God says about it. When you're in a fearful situation, you need people around who are able to speak truth to you.

Dave will say to me, "Now, let's stop for a moment." And that's what I'm saying to you. "Let's stop a moment and see what is the truth of the situation." Let's stop all this emotion. Let's stop this worry. Let's stop this fear. Let's go to the Word, and see what the truth of this matter is. I did that with my phone call situation and realized how easily I had followed this unhealthy thought process and hadn't stopped myself for a moment to ask, "What is the truth in this matter?" Decide that you're not going to believe a lie—whether about raising your children, about your marriage, about your finances, about your job, or about any situation. Decide instead to believe the truth and remove the glass ceiling.

And, you have the best help available to you. John 14:17 says, "The Spirit of Truth, whom the world cannot receive [and take to its heart] because it does not see Him or know Him, but you know Him because He (the Holy Spirit) remains with you continually and will be in you" (AMP). This is so beautiful. There is so much to the ministry of the Holy Spirit, but it's particularly comforting when Jesus says that the Spirit of Truth, the Holy Spirit, lives in you.

I want you to know that the Father sees you as an absolutely amazing person with outstanding potential because He sees you and me through the blood of Jesus. I want to encourage you to dig into the Word to see what God says about you. Then list anything that speaks against the way God sees you and start to dispel those lies, removing the glass ceiling in your life.

---

## PRIDE

Typically, when we hear *pride*, we think of magnifying ourselves and boasting of our strengths, which can be an issue. But what's more of a problem and causes more of a glass ceiling is exalting our abilities, or lack of them, over what Jesus did. If I took a test but didn't do very well, I might say, "I'm not going to take that test again. I can't do it because I didn't pass it last time. I'm just not that smart." But the Word of God says I have the mind of Christ. Which is true? Without pride, I would say, "I'm going to set aside my shortcomings, my past experience, and my natural limitations, and I'm going to believe what God said." Pride can mean believing your own limitations or what's only possible in the natural instead of believing what God says about the situation.

*Give it the best you have, but rely on the Lord to complete it and bring success. Stop looking at your own ability.*

Proverbs 11:2 says, "When pride comes [boiling up with an arrogant attitude of self-importance], then come dishonor and shame, but with the humble [the teachable who have been chiseled by trial and who have learned to walk humbly with God] there is wisdom and soundness of mind" (AMP). No matter your situation, you need to know that you can't do it without the Lord. Give it the best you have, but rely on the Lord to complete it and bring success. Stop looking at your own ability. God says in this verse that there's wisdom and soundness of mind when you humbly look to Him. I want to walk in wisdom and soundness of mind. The way to do that is to avoid self-reliance and self-righteousness but continually be humble in receiving what God has done for me.

Also in Proverbs, we see that "Pride goes before destruction, and a haughty spirit before a fall" (16:18, AMP). There are times I remind myself—especially during times of success—"Lord, I want to step back and acknowledge that this is not me, this is You. Help me steward the things You've put in front of me and the gifts and talents You've given me." I believe with that approach, God says, "Great! I can take you higher because I know you're not looking at yourself."

People who depend on themselves come quickly to the end of themselves. I don't want to have a glass ceiling that stops at my own natural talents and abilities. I want to honor God by receiving all He has for my life. A big part of that is seeing myself the way He sees me, but also knowing there are no limits on my life because He is near. When I don't depend on myself, there is peace and courage.

## ACTIVATION

What percentage of time do you find yourself focused on problems and difficulties? If your mind is focused on problems and difficulties, you probably have a glass ceiling in one of these areas.

What percentage of time do you hold yourself responsible for the results in your life? It's important that you don't see yourself as a victim but as a victor.

Are you consciously aware of the words you choose when talking to yourself? What are you saying to yourself about yourself? Your voice is one of the most powerful influences in your life.

What is the Holy Spirit saying to you about you? We know the Holy Spirit is going to speak in line with the truth of God's Word. Believe what He says.

## Taking the Limits Off Download:

https://drive.google.com/file/d/1ZSLHt0NHjBhOCvWooUF-8dDQ1sbS_GSS/view?usp=sharing

## Success Made Simple:

https://www.youtube.com/
playlist?list=PLuh1d30Agdvj7Vn3OAsnwKl2fsB1i2rtd

Chapter Six

# Discovering Your Purpose

D o you know anyone whose life has turned out the way he or she planned? I thought my life would be so much different for so many reasons. When my first husband, Tim, passed away suddenly, it was definitely not in my plans. However, living by the Word of God reveals that His plans are so much better than we can ever imagine for ourselves. Two years after Tim died, I quit my executive job and made plans to move with my son, Levi, to Colorado, where he felt called to attend Bible college. Levi had initially planned to go to school in Florida. He loves to surf, so being close to the ocean was on his bucket list. However, over the summer, Levi felt that God was calling him to go to Colorado, which is where the main campus location of Charis Bible College is located. During that visit, Levi heard God speak to his heart that if he was obedient and went to Colorado rather than Florida, God would bless him abundantly. Levi said yes to God, and we packed up everything with the help of friends and family and rented our house.

Renting the house would have been difficult in the natural, but God came through for us. We had quickly made our decision to

Your job is not your identity. But it can be one of the main ways God is able to fulfill your purpose.

move, and our home was an executive home that would rent for much higher than the median rental in the area. Because of this it generally takes weeks or even months to rent. I found a wonderful Christian property manager to list the home, and she already had a beautiful family looking for an executive rental to move into right away. God had taken care of finding us the perfect tenant! My parents and family had wondered what we were doing and why we would leave all our support systems that we had in Minnesota. My answer was that I knew the Lord was propelling me, and I needed to go.

## God knew I needed a God-given purpose to sustain me for what was ahead.

We moved to Colorado Springs feeling a bit like Abraham, not knowing where or what or how. All of my experience was in banking, but I couldn't get a banking job, no matter how hard I tried. I went from making $200,000 a year to making $10 per hour at the call center for Andrew Wommack Ministries. I went from running several divisions in three states with twenty-seven locations to having my phone calls recorded and critiqued by someone half my age.

I didn't know what was going on, but I did know enough to give everything I had where God placed me. At the time, I didn't realize that God was showing me how to dig in deep and find out why I was doing what I was doing. What were my motives, and were they in line with His plan? Was I going to do my job and apply my gifts and talents to climb the corporate ladder, be written up in the newspaper, or have a big paycheck?

God knew me so well. I needed to know I had a God-given purpose to sustain me for what He knew was ahead. During that time, I chose to be humbled. The Word of God tells us to humble ourselves. I needed to learn humility to be prepared for all He was bringing my way. The dreams and visions God gives are for an audience of One—Jesus Christ. Your call in life has everything to do with what Jesus has designed for you. When you find your purpose and really understand what it is that God sees in you, the ceiling in your life will be removed. When you understand your purpose and work for that audience of One, you can walk through anything with confidence and the expectation of success.

There are times in my life today when I laugh out loud because there's absolutely no way that anyone other than God could have put me in the positions I have held. In the past few years, I have pioneered multiple groundbreaking projects, products, and new business lines across multiple industries. Some of you may have heard of these projects and products but weren't aware that I was responsible for them behind the scenes. I have learned that position or prestige will never be the most important thing. Following what God has called you to do is the most important thing, and it empowers you to move and take mountains. Once you discover your purpose and allow God to help you recognize the gifts and talents He's given, you can purposely and systematically go boldly and confidently from glory to glory, wealthy place to wealthy place, living your life with excitement, joy, and peace. How does that sound?

*God has designed you with a unique purpose and destiny, but just knowing it's "out there" isn't enough.*

I am reminded of a time I attended a premier retail banking conference in Orlando, Florida. I went to learn best practices and innovative ideas to help bring our bank to the next level, as well as be more effective and successful in my position. The bank had spent a lot of money for me to attend the conference, and I wanted to provide a good return on their investment. I was inspired by the ideas and possibilities, but I quickly realized inspiration alone was not going to produce results. Unfortunately, no practical steps for implementing what I heard were provided. I left the conference disappointed, knowing that any benefit from the event would have to be produced on my own. Have you ever felt this way after hearing an inspiring sermon? There are wonderful promises of God spoken about, yet you have no idea how to get from where you are today to practically living those promises. I have been in this position many times, so in this chapter I'm going to provide some practical steps to help you discover your purpose.

It's encouraging to learn that God has designed you with a unique purpose and destiny, but just knowing it's "out there" isn't enough. I want to help you discover what His purpose is for your life. Proverbs 25:2 says, "It is God's privilege to conceal things and the king's privilege to discover them" (NLT). You are that king! It's your privilege to get with God to discover your purpose. God loves you so much, and He cherishes time and relationship with you. He wants to be involved in every area of your life, and your purpose is a vital part of your life.

This is an area very difficult to discover on your own. If you leave God out of the discovery process, you can't find what it is you are truly called to do. He designed your purpose specifically for you, and He already knows what it is. Get Him involved, and together you can uncover and discover your purpose. Now, let's prayerfully walk through questions directed toward helping you discover your purpose. I encourage you to take time to write out your answers, your thoughts, and your hopes. Pray over them and discuss them with someone who believes in you. This is going to be fun!

1.  **When looking at your life, what activities or jobs made you feel the most "alive" and successful?**

It may have nothing to do with the job or career you have currently. Many times, jobs or careers are chosen based on how successful or profitable they appear to be. Rarely are passions or contentment considered in choosing the direction for a career path. This was a very interesting question for me personally. I was not born again until I was thirty-one. Growing up, I went to church and knew about God. I think I loved God, but I didn't have a relationship with Him.

However, I can see His mercy as I look back on my life and think of all the places I worked and all the connections I made. Even without an understanding of God's purpose, He guided me, He put mentors in my path, and He provided me with excellent leadership. I'm able to glean from those years, even as I'm fulfilling God's purpose today. The leaders I worked with in banking and the processes I learned are valuable resources I still draw on. I didn't know my purpose, and I wasn't living for the Lord, but He was working on my behalf, preparing me for the future.

*It's encouraging to remember that we're called according to His plan and purpose, which He knows even if we don't.*

When the temptation comes to feel that you have wasted years and too many careers without knowing your purpose, take these words of encouragement to heart: "And we know [with great confidence] that God [who is deeply concerned about us] causes all things to work together [as a plan] for good for those who love God, to those who are called according to His plan and purpose" (Rom. 8:28, AMP). I live in this verse. Sometimes I can feel stress, discouragement, or doubt sneaking in, or I recognize I'm trying to take too much on myself. But even when I make mistakes, even when things don't go well, even when I'm struggling through a process, this verse always comforts me. It's encouraging to remember that I'm called according to His plan and purpose, which He knows even if I don't, and I'm doing my very best to live my life to fulfill it. What a comfort to have the confidence that He'll make all things work together for good.

Be encouraged! You can look back on your life, remove the things you know weren't of God, and see how He cared for you and led you through the years when you didn't realize it. It's a beautiful thread God has sewn through your life to get you where you are today, ready to step into your destiny. Look back and see how God was leading you, and pay attention to the things you learned. They will very likely have a major role in fulfilling your purpose today.

## 2. What are you able to accomplish easily but is often difficult for others?

This question will help you identify your gifts and talents. Sometimes you might think, *I'm really good at this without trying. Why does everyone else struggle with it?* I used to get frustrated with my employees and coworkers as a young leader when they couldn't catch on to concepts I was explaining. I just couldn't understand why they weren't "getting it." I was immature and unaware that God had blessed me with unique gifts and talents in these areas. You may have felt that way at some point too.

Proverbs 18:16 says that "A man's gift…makes room for him and brings him before great men" (AMP). This is the special endowment and grace that God has given you. For instance, it may be easy for you to look at a complex problem and immediately see how to solve it.

That would be a gift and talent. It may be you have a beautiful voice, while there are others of us who can't carry a tune. If you're one of those singers, recognize it as a gift and talent God has given you, and be aware that your purpose is probably tied to that gift. It's part of the uniqueness that is "the you" created by God. "Every good thing given and every perfect gift is from above; it comes down from the Father of lights [the Creator and Sustainer of the heavens], in whom there is no variation [no rising or setting] or shadow cast by His turning [for He is perfect and never changes]" (James 1:17, AMP). You will likely have many gifts on your list, and He promises to give you even more. Only a few will stand out as the core reason you do the things you do. Mark those core gifts in your notes, and begin asking the Lord how He can use them in your life.

# God thinks bigger than you do. He says His ways are not your ways.

God thinks bigger than you do. He says His ways are not your ways. That's not an insult; it's just that He is God, and He knows all things. The way He looks at things is not going to be the way you and I would naturally look at things until we transform our thinking by renewing our mind and thinking big like He thinks. Psalm 37:23 tells us that our steps are ordered by the Lord. "The steps of a good man are ordered by the Lord, and He delights in his way" (NKJV). That gives me confidence. Sometimes things in life don't make sense. It doesn't make sense if you struggle to see what He sees, so you need confidence that He has it all under control. God knows what is ahead of you, and He's already there, ordering your steps. As a child of God, you are able to seek Him and follow His voice and know that He has your whole path laid out. Isn't this good?

### 3. Under what circumstances do you quickly see solutions and feel compelled to take action?

My purpose is to *bring vision to reality*. If I'm talking to someone who starts to tell me about their vision and what God has put on their heart, I can't wait to get to work. I want to get out a piece of paper and start writing things down to help them bring their vision to reality. All the things I'm involved in contain an element of this purpose. For example, as a VP and Executive Marketing Director, my goal is to take the ministry's vision and bring it to reality. My mind continually pours out strategic plans and benchmark steps aimed toward fulfilling that vision. I absolutely love it.

When I was working in the phone center, God told me to start a home staging business and get my real estate license. Home staging is still a side business of mine. I have the same motivation in this business, although it may look different. When staging a home, I like to hear what the homeowner wants to see happen and help bring that vision for selling the home to reality. I once worked with a couple on a very large property. It was just the two of them after their children had moved, and the property had become a burden. They wanted to sell it to be free for travel and conduct mission work in Belize. For me, it wasn't about decorating a house, although I love that part, but it was about helping the homeowners' vision become a reality.

# *Purpose is what motivates me, and I apply vision to reality in every area of my life.*

Home staging is a lot of work. It includes hauling furniture, working for hours—sometimes through the night—renting moving vehicles, hiring movers, storing furniture, running to stores at the last minute to finish a job, and more. I learned that how I approached the job made all the difference. If my mindset going into a project was that it's simply a staging job I get paid to finish, I quickly found that the challenge of coordinating the move, moving furniture, packing up bins of décor, and putting up curtains wasn't worth all the work. I'd end up edgy and exhausted. However, if I took time to learn the vision of my clients and why they were selling the house, I put my heart into it, and it connected with my purpose. Purpose is what motivates me, and I apply vision to reality in every area of my life. Do you recognize similar areas in your life—areas where you see solutions or paths to success where others seem to be stuck?

"Listen carefully, I am about to do a new thing, now it will spring forth; will you not be aware of it? I will even put a road in the wilderness, rivers in the desert" (Isa. 43:19, AMP). What an encouraging Scripture! Sometimes when you receive an idea from the Lord, you're excited about it, but soon you can realize that you have no idea or no natural talent to execute it. That's when you need to do what this Scripture says and remind yourself of what the Lord told you. He's doing a new thing. It springs forth. Are you aware of it?

Ideas spring up, opportunities spring up, people we need to meet spring up. God wants us to have godly relationships. Most blessings come to us through other people. God is telling us through this verse to be aware of what He's causing to happen. It is a new thing. Then He's reminding us that He's making a way in the wilderness and streams in the desert. In other words, it might look impossible, but with Him all things are possible (see Matt. 19:26).

## 4.   What routine tasks bring you joy?

What do you love to do? What can you work on for hours and end up more energized than tired? "Whatever you do, work heartily, as for the Lord and not for men" (Col. 3:23, ESV). This is another clue to your purpose. God says He gives us the desires of our heart when we seek Him. He's not going to call you to spend your life doing something you hate to do. You can trust that those things which line up with the Word that you enjoy doing are from God. For me, I can work for hours staging a home. I worked on a home one day for fourteen hours! By the end of the day, I was physically tired, but I was not exhausted or drained. That's possible because I was working out of my purpose. I was loving every minute of fulfilling a purpose deeper than an individual job or assignment.

# God is not going to call you to spend your life doing something you hate to do.

There's a supernatural energy that comes to us from the Spirit of God when we live out His purpose. That energy is available to you. Think about what energizes you. It might not be related to anything you're involved with currently. Put this one in BIG letters in your notes.

5. **Have you ever held a job where you were content then later became discontent? What was the last project or assignment you mastered before becoming discontent?**

It's amazing how you can wake up one day and decide you're not being paid enough, and you're underappreciated or undervalued. I have lived this myself, and I realize now it's a warning sign. You may think earning more money will solve problems. It won't, and it doesn't bring satisfaction. When I hear people say they're not paid enough for what they're expected to do, it is a signal for me to ask, "Why are you feeling this way?" Usually it is masking a different problem. It's quite possible that they are no longer working from a healthy place. It could mean they have mastered their current task, which initially matched up to their purpose. Or, they may just need another challenge to continue to be fulfilled.

If you're starting to feel underappreciated, ask this question: "Am I working to please people or to please the Lord?" It's a good way to check whether you have gotten off track and have started pursuing recognition or money, which can creep up very subtly. Do any of these scenarios match the last time you felt discontent? Discontentment can also be an indication that there's a season of change or a transition coming your way.

*The Lord is always about growth, multiplication, fruitfulness, and profit.*

There can be multiple things God wants to shift in you during a season of change. Rarely is it just one area transitioning in our lives. "Thus says the Lord, your Redeemer, the Holy One of Israel: I am the Lord your God, Who teaches you to profit, Who leads you in the way that you should go. Oh, that you had hearkened to My commandments! Then your peace and prosperity would have been like a flowing river, and your righteousness [the holiness and purity of the nation] like the [abundant] waves of the sea" (Isa. 48:17-18, AMPC). When you and I are accustomed to hearing His voice and when your heart is striving after Him, you can understand what He's placing on your heart. It might be challenging, and you may feel fearful about the next season, but you can know your heavenly Father is always going to lead you into something greater. The Lord is always about growth, multiplication, fruitfulness, and profit. He'll always direct your life to the next level of grace, the next level of peace, and the next level of success.

### 6. What motivated you to make your last job or career change other than a pay increase?

When you have stepped out of or have not yet identified your purpose, you can feel unhappy in your job. Perhaps you completed an assignment within your purpose but received no additional assignments or challenges. Often these occurrences can trigger the idea of looking for another job. While you certainly may be called to move to another job, please take time to seek God and find out if this is indeed the situation. You may just need to make a course adjustment or a slight shift. Satisfaction comes from working out of your purpose. A little shift can put you back in line with your purpose in your current job, and there will be no need to make a career change.

You can apply this in every area of your life. When you're aware of your purpose, you can communicate with those in leadership openly. This is very helpful in the workplace. For example, now that I know what God has created me to do, I can go to my oversight team and say I need a new challenge. This is not based solely on my desires but on understanding my purpose and wanting to be more effective in my position. I can share my purpose with my supervisors, and together we can work on making sure I am applying my gifts and talents well. It also ensures that the Lord's purpose is not only being utilized to bring me satisfaction but to achieve goals for the business. If you're a leader or a parent, and you see this in your employees or children, take time to learn what their purpose is. Make sure you are giving them a challenge or an assignment where they are able to work on utilizing their purpose. What a joy it would be to help your children discover their purpose early in life.

*God has promised that He's given me the gifts and talents I need to fulfill my purpose.*

I get assignments daily that I have no idea how to accomplish. But what I do know is that God has promised that He's given me the gifts and talents I need to fulfill my purpose. He's done the same for you. If I'm given an assignment I know is from God, I can put my hand to it, trusting He has given me the gifts and talents I need to accomplish it. I don't need to know it in my head. I need to get it in my spirit. From this day forward, you can see things with your heart and not just your head. When you do, you will be on an adventure you never thought possible. God doesn't want you to accomplish things in your own strength. You get tired, weary, and manipulative. But when you know that everything He calls you to do is going to come from His strength and you cooperate with Him, you can start conquering those mountains.

7. **What current jobs, businesses, or activities do you feel are in line with God's purpose for your life?**

What do you like most about each one, and what is the common thread among them? Are there any that are unconnected, which you may need to stop doing? When you focus on doing what God has called you to do, you can expect the blessing of the Lord with no sorrow: "The blessing of the Lord—it makes [truly] rich, and He adds no sorrow with it [neither does toiling increase it]" (Prov. 10:22, AMPC). There are movie stars, music stars, executives, politicians, and more who hold on to their talent as their own. They seem to have achieved what everyone should want and strive after. So many people have found that seeking man's approval and positions without God's purpose leads to an empty and disappointing life. "For after all these things the Gentiles seek. For your heavenly Father knows that you need all these things. But seek first the kingdom of God and His righteousness, and all these things shall be added to you" (Matt. 6:32-33, NKJV). Strive after His purpose, and all the things the world pursues will be given to you, including peace. Evaluate your job, career, and activity choices through the filter of the Word of God and the direction of the purpose He has placed on your life. He will gladly guide you to the best place for you. (In your notes, document any volunteer or pro bono activities you're involved with, as well as your job, career, or educational training.)

God says in Matthew 25:29, as you value His gifts and apply them wisely, He will add to them, and you will be given more gifts. "For to everyone who has [and values his blessings and gifts from God, and has used them wisely], more will be given, and [he will be richly supplied so that] he will have an abundance; but from the one who does not have [because he has ignored or disregarded his blessings and gifts from God], even what he does have will be taken away" (AMP). If you don't apply His gifts wisely—if you're seeking the wrong things, being a poor steward, or doing nothing due to uncertainty—He says that even what you have will be taken away. I don't want to be in that situation; I want to be found faithful.

When God told me to start my home staging business, I did not have the gift of staging. I had never done it before in my life. But as I was ministering to people on the phone and applying the gifts and talents I had to what was in front of me, God dropped the gift of home staging and interior design into my spirit. I had nothing in the natural—no degree or training—to support home staging, only a word from God to do it. Three years later, I was featured on Lifetime's *Designing Spaces*, and I have published a book on home staging, *7 Seconds*. I can take no credit for it except my obedience. Because I valued and used my gifts, God gave me more gifts.

*God has purposely planted you where you are. You are not ordinary. You are extraordinary.*

Believe God to give you more gifts and talents as you are a wise and good steward with the gifts and talents you have. What gifts might be coming your way because of your faithfulness and your heart to serve His purpose? What you have today is not all God has for you. It is just the beginning.

I don't know what God has called you to do. But if you're reading this book, it's big. God has purposely planted you where you are. You are not ordinary. You are extraordinary. You are called to change the world, and He trusts you to step up and walk with Him. If you're able to get over your doubts and insecurities, God's plan for you is much bigger than what you could dream.

Living out of this place is incredible. God is utterly amazing. He is adventurous, and He wants to take you places you could never dream of going. You can imagine that someone like me, whose job it is to bring God's vision into a tangible reality for organizations and leaders, might make people uncomfortable. Implementing God's vision always includes change and moving people out of their comfort zone. Believe me, the resistance at times is intense, but it doesn't compare to the exhilaration of seeing a God-given vision come to pass.

Working out of your purpose provides an opportunity to live in perpetual success and satisfaction. "Many plans are in a person's mind, but the Lord's purpose will succeed" (Prov. 19:21, CEB). Not maybe, not might, but His purpose *will* succeed. When you line yourself up with God's purpose, success is imminent.

## ACTIVATION

After prayer and contemplating the questions in this chapter, complete the following sentence:

I am fulfilled, compelled, and gifted to…

_____

Congratulations! You have just discovered your purpose and put language to the desires you have held deep in your heart.

Discover Your Purposes Evaluation Download:

https://drive.google.com/file/d/1qsFxIzEm5WeHAvwvoI1Pkk-LHcnZuqDm/view?usp=sharing

# Chapter Seven

# Promises for Reaching Your Destiny

In the Introduction, I shared the story of Hagar who became an outcast and decided to flee her familiar surroundings because of Sarai's jealousy. In the wilderness, alone, pregnant, and vulnerable, she encountered the Angel of the Lord (Jesus), and being so moved by His love and compassion, she called Him, "the God who sees me." During her interaction with God, He spoke purpose over her life and blessed her and the son she had conceived.

Meanwhile in the camp, Abram and Sarai were discouraged and striving to believe the promise God had given them. Consistent with God's love and character, He didn't punish Abram and Sarai for taking matters into their own hands. There's great comfort in knowing that we aren't punished for our mistakes. Sarai did eventually conceive a son with Abram named Isaac, which means "laughter," who became a great nation and a blessing to all generations. God continued to faithfully interact with them and changed their names to match their destiny before they ever saw the physical manifestation. Abram, meaning "exalted father" became Abraham, meaning "father of a multitude." And Sarai, or "princess," became Sarah, meaning "noblewoman."

God has made you a blessing in your community. He has given you all the territory you can see.

God communicated to Abraham the details of his blessed life, and they have become the foundations of our faith. The blessings and promises He gave Abraham and Sarah were for vision and empowerment to live out their purpose. These same promises are available for you to fulfill your own purpose.

The blessings of Abraham are vast and far-reaching. God already has blessed your family, your name, and your children. He promises protection, provision, and authority. You can be fruitful, righteous, and a blessing to the nations. You qualify for all the blessings of Abraham through the blood of Jesus. All this and more is available for you because Jesus has already made provision. All you need to do to receive is believe.

Galatians explains that God freed us from the curse and positioned us to receive all the promises and blessings He made in times past: "Christ redeemed us from the curse of the law by becoming a curse for us—for it is written, 'Cursed is everyone who is hanged on a tree'—so that in Christ Jesus the blessing of Abraham might come to the Gentiles, so that we might receive the promised Spirit through faith" (Gal. 3:13-14, ESV).

The covenant was with Jesus and the promises made to Him. Because we are in Him, we qualify to participate in the covenant. We have a covenant of peace, sealed by the blood of Jesus, and our actions will not change the covenant.

I've compiled a list of the blessings of Abraham that will encourage your faith and remind you of the things you already hold in your hand as you step into your destiny and purpose. My heart's desire is that these promises will be a source of faith and strength to help you boldly step with confidence into all God has before you.

---

**He made you a great nation (Gen. 12:2).**

God says you are a great nation. This was a blessing spoken over Abraham. What does it mean to be a great nation? I like to look at my family as a great and mighty nation. All the lineage, all the generations that will come through Levi, I declare and believe will be great. Receive it for yourself. It is done.

**He made your name great (Gen. 12:2).**

There are times in life you can feel nobody knows who you are or cares if you exist. But through the blessing of Abraham, God says He has already made your name great. If you're feeling overlooked or you're not doing anything to leave a legacy, that's not what God says about you. Declare today that He has made your name great. You don't need to fight or muster up the faith to make it happen. You can receive it and know your name is great. Declare over yourself and your family that your name is great!

**He made you to be a blessing (Gen. 12:2).**

I love this because if I enter a situation where I'm challenged and feeling ungenerous, God says He has made me to be a blessing. I can adjust my heart, knowing I've already been made a blessing for others. One of the things I hear particularly from women—whether single, divorced, or widowed—is they don't want to be a bother to anyone. Can you relate? I can't tell you how many conversations I have been in similar to the one I had with a friend the other day. She was helping with my hair and makeup and said, "Karen, anytime you need help, please let me know." I heard myself say, "I just don't want to be a bother." I never want to be a bother. But I need to stop thinking that way and understand that I'm not a bother; I'm a blessing. When you feel like a bother, you walk timidly into a room, you don't call people for help, and you don't want to disturb anyone. God doesn't want that for you. He wants you to understand that even in a crowd, He's already declared you to be a blessing.

Try walking into your workplace with this understanding. I had some small, challenging things come up over the last few days at work, and I can tell you that I wasn't feeling like a blessing. I know when I start to work or interact with people feeling that I'm a bother and not a blessing, my actions unconsciously follow my feelings. Declare today that you are a blessing because He made you to be a blessing, which absolutely includes prosperity and great favor.

# God is looking to bless all those around us.

**He blesses those who bless you (Gen. 12:3).**

This is so awesome because it means when people help me, bless me, speak good things over me, give me gifts, or spend time with me, God will bless them in return. I thank God that because they chose to bless me, He is going to bless them. What an empowered way to live. What if you approached each day this way? Say you went into the grocery store, and the clerk was nice to you. You can walk away knowing that because the clerk blessed you, God will bless the clerk. I love this because it shares the heart of God. He rewards people who bless His children. You can expect blessing, and you can receive blessing. God is looking to bless all those around us.

## He curses those who curse you (Gen. 12:3).

You are not under the curse, and God is not in the cursing business, but there's something here that shows God is looking out for you. If someone says or does something unkind, you can know that He cares about it, and He takes it personally. You can go to Him and trust Him to get you through difficult times.

## He made all the families of the earth blessed in you (Gen. 12:3).

That means all the families of the earth are going to be blessed through those who belong to Jesus Christ. When you have children, you can know that your children are blessed. God has a plan on the earth to expand His kingdom through your family. Teach your children about the Lord and train them at a young age. His influence will spread to the ends of the earth through your family.

## He gave you and your descendants land (Gen. 12:7).

I teach a lot on real estate. There are many Christians right now who feel called or directed by the Holy Spirit to be active in the real estate market. Why is that? I believe it's biblical because the earth is made up of land that mankind was given dominion and ownership over (see Gen. 1:26). You are to have land and to have some control over what happens on that land. If you've never owned land or you feel God doesn't want you to own a house, I can tell you He does. And He has already made provision for it. Praise God, He has given you land.

## He gave you and all your descendants all the land you can see (Gen. 13:14-15).

He didn't just give you land but all the land you can see. This goes beyond ownership; it speaks to the godly influence you have with your neighbors and community. The promises to Abraham went beyond the physical realm and had spiritual implications that he understood. Hebrews 11:10 explains that Abraham was looking for a city with eternal foundations designed and built by God. He realized his forever home was not earth and that he was an influencer in society over a geographical area that God identified. We too have a dual perspective of earthly influence with an eternal emphasis as a follower of Jesus.

This blessing gives me faith that I can make an impact on the people around me. You are to be a blessing in your community. Take hold of the Word of God, and make sure that the people in relationship with you and living around you see you representing God. You are a light in your community and neighborhood, and God has given you the land.

*You can make an impact on the people around you. You are made to be a blessing in your community.*

**He gave you descendants numerous as the dust of the earth (Gen. 13:16).**

I love this too, and of course Abraham saw his descendants as the sand on the shore. God told him he was going to have all these descendants, even though he didn't have any children at the time. Abraham received God's promise by faith. I want to encourage you that if you're believing God for children, it is a blessing of Abraham. You will have children in Jesus' name.

**He is a shield for you (Ps. 5:12).**

As you go through life, there can be some dangerous times. I had a situation recently where I was driving just outside my workplace, and I felt this little bump with my car. I looked up, and it was a big buck. I just caught a glimpse of it. Hitting a deer can be dangerous, but God protected me, and the buck kept running. When I looked at the front of my car, I saw that my headlights were all pushed in. People stopped me in the driveway of the building where I work, concerned about what had happened. I said that I hit a deer, but it was just a little bump. They were stunned because it looked so serious, and I could have been injured.

When I called the insurance company and told them what happened, I explained the damage, and they were concerned I had whiplash or back issues. I told them I was fine. God was my shield. He's my shield in the natural, but He's also a shield in the spiritual realm. When there are times I don't know if I can be brave enough to step out into something or I have a challenge I can't quite figure out, God is my shield. God is a shield for your family as well. I know that I can have faith because the Word says it's a blessing of Abraham for me.

*He's my shield in the natural, but He's also a shield in the spiritual realm.*

**He made your reward very great (Gen. 15:1).**

God is a God of reward. He rewards those who diligently seek Him (see Heb. 11:6). When I do things that I know are between God and me, things no one else can see but God has prompted me to do, I can be assured He has already made my reward great. When Levi let me know he was called to go to Bible college, that was not anything I had expected. We knew that if he was going to go to Bible college it would be Charis Bible College because that was the college we trusted.

When he felt that the Lord spoke to him and said he was to go look at Charis in Colorado, we drove fifteen hours to visit the campus, even though Levi's heart was still on the ocean and surfing. At the time, Levi didn't know why God said that if he went to Colorado instead of Florida He would reward him, but all through those years we hung on to that word. Because Levi was obedient to go to Colorado, God faithfully blessed him over and over. Even today, Levi leans on that word and reminds the Lord, "You told me to go to Colorado, and I know that I've got a blessing coming." You and I can be assured that because we are the seed of Abraham, He has promised that our reward would be very great.

**He established a covenant with you (Gen. 17:7).**

# God never takes His covenant with you and me lightly.

This is huge. God established a covenant with you. When you make a covenant with God, He doesn't back out just because you've had a bad day. He doesn't decide that He doesn't like you one day, so He's going to break covenant with you. Marriage in our society is a covenant, but we have begun to take it lightly. God never takes His covenant with you and me lightly. You have assurance when you receive Jesus Christ that you are in covenant with God, and He'll never break that covenant.

## He multiplied you exceedingly (Gen. 22:17).

This could mean prosperity with finances; He might have multiplied your peace, multiplied your joy, or multiplied your family. God is into multiplication. First Corinthians 3:7 says that you and I plant and we water, but all the while God gives the increase. Where do you need increase today? Say out loud: "God, You have already multiplied me in this area because these are the blessings of Abraham, and they are mine. I will begin to walk in Your success."

## Kings come forth from you (Gen. 17:6).

You are kings and priests through Jesus Christ. You and I are royalty. Not according to the world's standards, but you are royalty according to God's standards. Here is a practical application of royalty: When a king declares something and it leaves his mouth, it is done. There are people in the kingdom who follow through with what he declares. As you and I declare the Word of God and speak things in line with the Word of God, we are agreeing with God, and as kings we know it must be done. We don't control people, but we have authority in our lives, and no one can stop the blessings of God in our life.

Only you can decide if you're going to let someone else or the enemy or circumstances stop you. The Word of God is true, and let every man be a liar. When you see yourself as a king and you picture yourself giving a decree—declaring something over your kingdom—you can trust you have authority and things will happen according to the Word of God. Knowing this also makes me aware that I need to watch what I speak. I want to speak life over myself, my family, and the people I work with. You are a king, and your children are royalty.

**He made you exceedingly fruitful (Gen. 17:6).**

When I go to work and I have a whole list of things I need to do, I am so happy He has already made me fruitful. When I start to work on something, even if I don't know exactly what I'm going to be doing, I can declare and agree that I am exceedingly fruitful. I'll just say, "Lord, I don't know exactly what all I have to get done today, but You have promised me through the blessing of Abraham that I will be fruitful, and I want my fruit to last." When you do something fruitful, you can trust God to multiply it and know it is going to last. I love that part of the blessing. You can teach your children that they are fruitful. They can know how important they are to God and that they can do anything in Christ.

*We can help young people receive an identity and know they are contributing to society.*

My son was sharing with me a podcast of a famous psychologist teaching at a college. He was trying to understand why we have young people, who are really bright and making things happen—hustling, working, living for God—and then there seems to be a whole segment who are unproductive, depressed, and have low self-esteem.

The world is working overtime to convince young people that despite any of their behavior, they are okay—no matter what state they're in. Yet when this professor asked how many felt they were being wasteful with their time, without providing any definition of wasteful, there was a significant percentage who self-identified and raised their hand. Those young people know better. God has given us a conscience. They know they are not walking in a healthy way. They know they're not being fruitful.

What if we spoke to these young people and let them know they were created to be fruitful? They are created to make a difference. We can help young people receive an identity and know they are contributing to society. When you raise your children, teach them that God has made them exceedingly fruitful. Agree with God that He has made you and your family fruitful. When I put in a good day of work, when I get a house done and see it is a blessing and it is fruitful, I am happy. He has given you these promises to know who you are in Christ.

## He has given you righteousness (Gen. 15:6).

He has made you in right standing with God, and it isn't based on your behavior. It isn't because you're so smart. You are the righteousness of God because you have received Jesus Christ, and this is one of the blessings of Abraham. You can hold your head high and come boldly to the throne of grace to receive mercy and find grace to help in your time of need (see Heb. 4:16).

We receive grace through faith (belief). Faith is a personal belief, a persuasion, an assurance, and a response to God's character and dependability that results in trust. Faith is in harmony with grace because it involves trusting God's gift of unmerited favor. Grace becomes available when your belief (faith) is aligned and in harmony with God. Grace comes to us the moment we believe in our heart at salvation, and it continues to operate from our faith.

You can go to your Father, who is God and has made all the universe. He knows you, and when He looks at you He sees you as righteous as Jesus. That is amazing. You are able to take His robe of righteousness and walk on this earth as if you are sinless.

## He has made you to father a multitude of nations (Gen. 17:4).

We want every nation to know Jesus. He has already made you a father to a multitude of nations. You can believe He has made it possible for every nation, tongue, and tribe to come to know the name of Jesus.

## He has established His covenant between me, you, and your seed forever (Gen. 31:44).

When God established a covenant with you through Jesus Christ, it wasn't just for this moment. You can stand on the Word and know all the generations behind you are going to be in covenant with God. You can stand in faith and start to speak it out. I can have my grandchildren sit on my lap and tell them they are in covenant with a good Father. The first person in the family who decides to receive Jesus Christ can change a lineage and a family forever. My first husband, Tim, was one of those. He received Jesus Christ when his family did not have a relationship with Jesus. They went to church, but they didn't understand who they were in Christ. They also had alcoholism and abuse in the family, which was not a good situation. Tim could have believed that this was just how it was for him, but instead he made a decision to receive Jesus Christ. The Conrad lineage is changed forever because of that decision.

Now with your children, your children's children, and even the generations you won't know until you see them in heaven, you can declare over them and know that they will serve God. They are in covenant throughout all the generations. That is great news when you're a mama with a heart for your children. You can be excited for the day you have grandchildren. This ministers to me because I know I can trust God not only with my son but with my future grandchildren and my great-grandchildren. That is a blessing of Abraham.

## He will be God to you and your descendants (Gen. 17:7).

He will be your God. God is a big God, and you can go to Him for anything you need. He says, "I will be your God." He never breaks a promise and never leaves your side. The comfort of such everlasting love is boundless.

**He has greatly blessed you (Gen. 12:2).**

This isn't something you have to ask for. You don't have to beg God to bless you. No, He has greatly blessed you today in every area of your life. It is a done deal based on His faithfulness.

**He has greatly multiplied your seed (Gen. 16:10).**

You will have generations and generations, and your family will not pass out of remembrance. Your seed will last for multiplied generations.

**He has made you and your descendants possess the enemy's gates (Gen. 22:17).**

*Possessing the enemy's gate means the enemy cannot gain entrance to you or your family.*

This is powerful. Sometimes you may think your enemies are other people, but we don't fight against flesh and blood. There is one enemy, the devil, but God says that no matter what comes against you or tries to harm you and your family, He has already possessed the enemy's gates. If you've possessed the enemy's gate, the enemy cannot gain entrance to you or your family. That is powerful, and He has given that to you through the blessings of Abraham.

## He has blessed many nations through you and your seed (Deut. 15:6).

Not only are your children and grandchildren blessed, but through them many nations are blessed. That means they're going to carry the Word of God into many nations. God could give one of your children a cure for cancer. Through works of faith in God, through your jobs, through preaching and teaching, God will bless many nations through your seed.

Through the blessings of Abraham, we have all these things and so much more. Following is a list of promises (not anywhere near comprehensive) that gets me excited whenever I think about them. The Word of God is not a list of rules but a manual for living an abundant life. It's a treasure chest of gifts and promises to help fulfill your purpose. In it you'll find answers to every question and tools for every situation. And there's power to overcome right at your fingertips. Let's talk about what you already have in your hands.

### Favor and Good Understanding

*And so find favor and high esteem in the sight of God and man* (Proverbs 3:4, NKJV).

## God and His Word Are True

*By no means! Let God be true though every one were a liar, as it is written, "That you may be justified in your words, and prevail when you are judged"* (Rom. 3:4, ESV).

## He Is Ready to Fulfill His Word

*Then the Lord said to me, "You have seen well, for I am ready to perform My word"* (Jeremiah 1:12, NKJV).

## No Weapon Formed Against Us Will Prosper

*"No weapon formed against you shall prosper, and every tongue which rises against you in judgment you shall condemn. This is the heritage of the servants of the Lord, and their righteousness is from Me," says the Lord* (Isaiah 54:17, NKJV).

## Perfect Peace for Those Focusing on Him

*You will keep him in perfect peace, whose mind is stayed on You, because he trusts in You* (Isaiah 26:3, NKJV).

## Prosperity Like a Tree Planted by Water

*He is like a tree planted by streams of water that yields its fruit in its season, and its leaf does not wither. In all that he does, he prospers* (Psalm 1:3, ESV).

## The Steps of a Righteous Man Are Ordered by God

*The steps of a man are established by the Lord, when he delights in his way; though he fall, he shall not be cast headlong, for the Lord upholds his hand* (Psalm 37:23-24, ESV).

## Peaceful Direction in Life

*Trust in the Lord with all your heart, and lean not on your own understanding; in all your ways acknowledge Him, and He shall direct your paths* (Proverbs 3:5-6, NKJV).

## A Life Full of Blessing

*Praise the Lord! (Hallelujah!) Blessed [fortunate, prosperous, and favored by God] is the man who fears the Lord [with awe-inspired reverence and worships Him with obedience], who delights greatly in His commandments. His descendants will be mighty on earth; the generation of the upright will be blessed. Wealth and riches are in his house, and his righteousness endures forever. Light arises in the darkness for the upright; He is gracious and compassionate and righteous (upright—in right standing with God)* (Psalm 112:1-4, AMP).

## He Has Appointed My Times and Purpose

*For he will complete what he appoints for me, and many such things are in his mind* (Job 23:14, ESV).

## Wisdom and Revelation

*That the God of our Lord Jesus Christ, the Father of glory, may give you the Spirit of wisdom and of revelation in the knowledge of him* (Ephesians 1:17, ESV).

## Purpose for Living

*For we are his workmanship, created in Christ Jesus for good works, which God prepared beforehand, that we should walk in them* (Ephesians 2:10, ESV).

## Victory and Success

*Now to him who is able to do far more abundantly than all that we ask or think, according to the power at work within us, to him be glory in the church and in Christ Jesus throughout all generations, forever and ever. Amen* (Ephesians 3:20-21, ESV).

## Relationship with the Father

*For it is God who works in you, both to will and to work for his good pleasure* (Philippians 2:13, ESV).

## Power to Get Wealth

*And you shall remember the Lord your God, for it is He who gives you power to get wealth, that He may establish His covenant which He swore to your fathers, as it is this day* (Deuteronomy 8:18, NKJV).

# FAITH-BASED RIGHTEOUSNESS

I'm so glad that we don't have to earn our righteousness. It simply comes through faith in what Jesus did in His death and resurrection. Isn't it interesting that Abraham had a revelation of this in the Old Testament? The apostle Paul explained in Romans 4:13-25 that Abraham was the receiver of righteousness and promises by faith. He said that Abraham, in hope, believed. Righteousness through faith was a message that Paul taught, along with his message of grace and peace, and that really upset the religious leaders of his day. Paul taught people to stop trying to earn their righteousness and simply receive it through faith in what Jesus did. The peace and love of God is available to us because of Jesus' completed work, not our performance. The religious leaders of Paul's day wanted to "earn" God's approval and blessings. They couldn't humble themselves to receive it freely as a gift. It became an offense, a stumbling stone to Paul's message of the gospel. When we understand that righteousness is a gift we receive by faith, it opens up an entirely new way of living.

*The peace and love of God is available to us because of Jesus' completed work, not our performance.*

So now you may be asking, how do I muster up enough faith to attain this amazing gift? I have more good news for you. You don't have to strive for enough faith; God made provision for you. Hebrews 12:1-3 explains that Jesus is actively involved in our faith from the beginning to the end. Hebrews 12:2 describes Jesus as the "author and perfecter" of our faith. The definition of *author* in Greek is "captain." That helps us understand that Jesus was the originator of our faith because He begins it, and then leads it as a captain leads a ship and cares for it. The word *perfecter* in verse 2 means "finish." We can trust Jesus to bring our faith to conclusion. This is so wonderful!

When I feel that my faith is not as strong as it should be, I lean into this Scripture and ask Jesus to make up any lack in my faith and bring it to completion for me. Jesus, the Captain of our faith, watches over us, cares for us, and sustains us. You may recall the story about Hagar and her experience with the angel of the Lord. He saw her, showed up to care for her, and spoke purpose over her, which sustained her.

You can take God's Word and believe it above any thought or circumstance coming your way. Entertaining thoughts that don't line up with the Word of God give an access point to negativity and produce unhealthy behaviors. God has so much more reserved for you, and He is near to help you navigate your journey with purpose. He has made provision for you in every area of your life, and His Word is the manual for success. He has promises and blessings stored up for you that are astounding.

## ACTIVATION

Take some time to read the stories of the heroes found in the Hall of the Faith (Hebrews 11). They were just regular people with difficulties and flaws, but they believed God would do what He said He would do. When their lives were remembered, inspired by the Holy Spirit, nothing negative was recorded about them—only their trust in God and their accomplishments. With that in mind, write down what you believe God would say about your life.

| | |
|---|---|
| **Abel:** | He gave his offering by faith. |
| **Enoch:** | He pleased God. (Without faith it is impossible to please God. See Hebrews 11:6.) |
| **Noah:** | He built the ark by faith, having never seen rain. |
| **Abraham:** | He left his home by faith without knowing his destination. |
| **Sarah:** | She received strength by faith to conceive Isaac, the child of promise. |
| **Abraham:** | He offered Isaac by faith, knowing God had promised a nation through him. |
| **Isaac and Jacob:** | They blessed their sons by faith for promised things to come. |
| **Moses:** | By faith, his parents defied Pharaoh; by faith, he refused to deny his people; by faith, he led the children of Israel out of Egypt; by faith, they walked through the Red Sea. |

What are you believing God for today that has been provided through the blessings of Abraham? Make a list of those things, along with the Scripture that provides for the situation, and write them out as a declaration of faith.

God's Blessing of Faith Scriptures Download:

https://drive.google.com/file/d/1Y57HBbFUCrsaGgFUN5hq_UE-w0PYdkxl/view?usp=sharing

Look at challenges you face on a daily basis through the lens of the Word of God.

# Chapter Eight

# Tools to Fulfill Your Purpose

I've been working with a large organization for about two years now. It has become one of the most challenging yet exciting opportunities I've been given to apply my God-given purpose of bringing vision to reality. When I started my job, there was no clear path on what to do, or how to do it, or even what we were trying to accomplish. It was initially uncomfortable for someone like me, who likes clear paths. I'm a person who likes to know how success is defined—the vision that I'm going to bring to reality—and there were no clear documented goals for what I was hired to do. This went against everything I knew and gained satisfaction from in the corporate world. It quickly became another adventure with God that was going to stretch me once again.

"Practice what you preach" became my mantra. Seek God on where to focus, and trust Him to make a way in the wilderness and rivers in the desert (see Isa. 43:6). I didn't know the target I was trying to hit, so it was an exercise in trusting God daily and taking the steps I felt led to take. I did my best to apply general biblical keys to success gleaned over the years then just release the rest to God. The results? Amazing! Much better than I could have imagined!

Principles for success, whether personal or business related, can ultimately be traced back to the Bible. You will find that God is very invested in your success, and He provides you with all the tools, talents, and grace you need. "For the Lord gives wisdom; from His mouth come knowledge and understanding" (Prov. 2:6, NKJV). In my more than thirty years of business and ministry experience, I have collected a few pieces of wisdom I like to call keys to success or best practices. These are simple things you deal with on a daily basis, and when you add them up, they will head you in the direction of peace and success. You no doubt want to be successful in your career, business, marriage, and family. These keys can be learned, practiced, and applied in every area of your life with time-tested results. Let's dig in!

## ENTHUSIASM CAN BE CONTAGIOUS

**You can influence and attract others and be a change maker in your sphere.**

Think about a time in your home or office when the atmosphere needed to change. Have you ever had enthusiastic teachers or colleagues change the atmosphere in the room because their passion for the subject or confidence in the team became contagious? Scripture indicates that it all starts with delighting in the Lord and His Word. "Blessed [fortunate, prosperous, and favored by God] is the man who fears the Lord [with awe-inspired reverence and worships Him with obedience], who delights greatly in His commandments" (Ps. 112:1, AMP). This is only one verse, but I encourage you to read the whole chapter.

As leader of an organization, team, or family, if you approach the office, a Zoom call, or a meeting with a lack of enthusiasm, how can you expect the people around you to be encouraged or upbeat? Galatians 6:9-10 says, "And let us not grow weary of doing good, for in due season we will reap, if we do not give up. So then, as we have opportunity, let us do good to everyone, and especially to those who are of the household of faith" (ESV).

*With enthusiasm, you can overcome obstacles that would otherwise feel impossible.*

On the positive side, let me give you an example. Recently, I was leading a project where we ran into some deadlines and problems, putting the entire project at risk. Several steps were required to get this project back on track. I knew that whatever attitude I had was going to carry over to the team. I knew I needed to go into our conference call with enthusiasm and courage, despite the obstacles and challenges. I could encourage the team to complete the four or five things outlined and propose we could certainly hit the deadline. Or the opposite—I could take the call lacking enthusiasm and communicate that the deadline was impossible to meet due to the work required. The people looking to me for leadership and hope would literally have to fight against the atmosphere I had created to be able to hit the deadline and accomplish what we all wanted to achieve. In that situation of bringing enthusiasm to the group, I gave them hope and lifted the energy level. The entire team left the meeting feeling that they could handle the task ahead.

With enthusiasm, you can overcome obstacles that would otherwise feel impossible. I want to encourage you to come with enthusiasm to your leadership role, whether of your family or your colleagues. When you do, you will find other people enjoy being around you.

## FORCE OF HABIT

**Your life is a result of what you do daily. It all begins one day at a time.**

Sometimes you don't want to hear that, because frankly there are days you would really like to sit around and not accomplish a lot. And one day every once in a while is not a problem, but regular, daily, negative habits are. Galatians 6:7 tells us, "Do not be deceived: God is not mocked, for whatever one sows, that will he also reap" (ESV).

Dave and I try to watch what we eat and stay away from sugar. We were in a habit of not eating sweets and found we didn't miss sugar much. Then we went on a mini-vacation, and a friend recommended a place that made great chocolate crepes. When we arrived, we found the restaurant, but crepe season was over. However, they had incredible brownies, which we decided to try. We had developed a habit of generally avoiding desserts, but we were going to enjoy the brownie on our cheat day. So, we ate the brownie, and it was good. But then we had a dinner party a few days later at a friend's house with a lovely meal and special ice cream purchased from Santa Ana, California. We would normally have passed, but that night we looked at each other and said, "Let's try it!" Before I knew it, we had stopped our habit of no sugar, and we were having sweets three times that week. We realized we were going to have to back off on the sweets because it had started to become a habit.

Now again, there's nothing wrong with eating sweets once in a while, and I don't mean to make a big deal about food. I'm just making a point about allowing things in our lives on a consistent basis. Sometimes it can start to become our habit, even if we don't see it ourselves. We saw ourselves eating healthy, but we were making exceptions on a daily basis, making the exceptions a habit. There are some things we all do every day that we may need to stop doing.

Then there are some things we don't do every day that we may want to start doing. There are productive habits we can incorporate that bring life on a daily basis. "One who is faithful in a very little is also faithful in much, and one who is dishonest in a very little is also dishonest in much" (Luke 16:10, ESV). An example of someone who accomplished amazing things set in place by a daily habit is John Maxwell. Maxwell is one of the greatest authors on leadership in the world, having written nearly 100 books on the subject.

So what's the secret to someone being able to write that many books? My husband had the opportunity to sit with him at lunch one day and asked him. How are you able to write so many books? John explained to Dave that he disciplines himself to write daily for at least thirty minutes. He writes down his thoughts on a subject, and then later hands the compiled material over to an assistant who works with him. That person takes the information, sorts, and edits it into order for future books. All the information is coming out of John as the author, born out of a daily habit of writing a little bit every day. That was encouraging to me because writing a book or sitting down and writing several pages on a report can honestly be overwhelming. But anybody can take fifteen minutes a day and write. "His master said to him, 'Well done, good and faithful servant. You have been faithful over a little; I will set you over much. Enter into the joy of your master'" (Matt. 25:21, ESV).

*There are productive habits we can incorporate that bring life on a daily basis.*

---

### DEVELOP A POSITIVE MENTAL ATTITUDE

**You cannot control what other people do, but you can control how you respond. Negativity steals hope.**

---

One of the keys to maintaining a positive attitude is to listen to things, read things, and pay attention to things that are positive around you. How is that possible when there is so much negative attitude and information out there? You learn to look at things through the lens of God's Word. You can even look at challenges you face on a daily basis, believing God is in control and has the best life planned for you. Philippians 4:8-9 tells us how to do this: "Finally, brothers, whatever is true, whatever is honorable, whatever is just, whatever is pure, whatever is lovely, whatever is commendable, if there is any excellence, if there is anything worthy of praise, think about these things. What you have learned and received and heard and seen in me—practice these things, and the God of peace will be with you" (ESV). When you look at things with a positive mental attitude, it gives you an incredible edge, and you are a much happier person.

*When you look at things with a positive mental attitude, it gives you an incredible edge, and you are a much happier person.*

---

Being an agent of change myself, I frequently work toward bringing change through alternative techniques and fresh ideas. Change usually requires doing things differently, and not everyone is happy about change. There are many who will openly speak out about the change and question the new direction you've implemented. I have learned not to stew about things like this but to develop a positive mental attitude toward these situations.

Even though it's discouraging initially, I've found if I look with a positive mental attitude, realizing that change is hard for people, I can see the whole situation differently. Instead of getting upset at someone resisting my changes, I see it as helping me identify someone who needs more clarity to understand the process and the steps being taken toward the final goal. It's helpful to find those people, then take a moment to talk to them rather than submit to the temptation to do something just to make myself look good. Proverbs 16:24 says, "Gracious words are like a honeycomb, sweetness to the soul and health to the body" (ESV). Or, in other words, you can catch more flies with honey than with vinegar.

During my life, I have endured betrayal, lies to and about me, theft, slander, false accusation, disappointment, and sorrow. Although these were sad moments, I've still had much more joy than sorrow! Often, it made people angrier that I remained positive, but a positive mental attitude is what got me through these things and more without offense, bitterness, or anger. I had a boss tell me one time, "Karen, you are stronger than ten acres of garlic!" I think that was a compliment. What made me appear so strong? Living out this key and believing that the Word is true. "And we know that for those who love God all things work together for good, for those who are called according to his purpose" (Rom. 8:28, ESV).

---

### MAKE A COMMITMENT TO EXCELLENCE

**Be prepared to pay the full price for excellence, and count the cost.**

---

I have to work at this one pretty consistently, and I will tell you why. I like to get things done and done quickly. Every day, I see another reason why God brought Dave and me together. He helps remind me that we need to do things with excellence. We've been doing some projects around the house, and one is whitewashing over orange brick then painting the floor gray on our porch. In my enthusiasm, I wanted it done quickly. As Dave walked me through all the necessary steps in preparation for the paint, I appreciated that he wanted to do the job right, not just get it done fast. We have a push-pull in our relationship that I *mostly* love. Things may take just a little longer to get done in the house, but the result is always better, and it's done with excellence. That has been exceedingly helpful for me. "Whatever you do, work heartily, as for the Lord and not for men, knowing that from the Lord you will receive the inheritance as your reward. You are serving the Lord Christ" (Col. 3:23-24, ESV).

*Excellence usually requires extra time and extra effort, but the result is worth it in every area.*

Excellence usually requires extra time and extra effort, but the result is worth it in every area. Good examples of this are proofing what you write before you send it, pausing and not rushing an emotional response, looking through things produced like a newsletter and making sure all the information is correct, or checking grammar when documenting a written process. All these things can help assure you're going to develop the best opportunity for excellence. Not everyone is gifted in the area of details. I can look at details if I need to, but it's difficult for me. Because I don't like to look at details—I'm not very good at it—I like to surround myself with people who love details. You can utilize these keys, but you don't have to accomplish all of them yourself. By being aware of them, you can surround yourself with a team or put processes in place to help leverage these keys for success. In the areas where you're not as strong, you can find a team member who is.

"By faith Abel offered to God a more acceptable sacrifice than Cain, through which he was commended as righteous, God commending him by accepting his gifts. And through his faith, though he died, he still speaks" (Heb. 11:4, ESV). Long-term, you're always going to be happier doing things with excellence. I want to encourage you that this is one of those key areas you can bring people around you. Pull the gifts and talents out of those in your family, your spouse, and your colleagues at work. Hire people who can fill gaps for you. The spirit of excellence is something that pleases God because it reflects His Spirit.

---

### DEVELOP PERSISTENCE AND PERSEVERANCE

This comes through enduring difficulties. Struggle develops character.

---

One of the examples I like to use for perseverance is starting a business or ministry. What if, after ten years, there hasn't been much difficulty or any major issues to work through? The prevailing mindset would be a false sense that everything is going to be perfect. But after significant growth, challenges start to arise. Unfortunately, you wouldn't know how to handle them. Dealing with challenges is cumulative. You must build up to it.

"And not only this, but [with joy] let us exult in our sufferings and rejoice in our hardships, knowing that hardship (distress, pressure, trouble) produces patient endurance; and endurance, proven character (spiritual maturity); and proven character, hope and confident assurance [of eternal salvation]. Such hope [in God's promises] never disappoints us, because God's love has been abundantly poured out within our hearts through the Holy Spirit who was given to us" (Rom. 5:3-5, AMP).

*Going through difficult times helps you gain strength.*

As you gain influence moving toward your mission or vision, you're going to face opposition. That certainly was true in the life of Jesus and His disciples. If the disciples had not encountered challenges along the way, it would have been much more difficult for them after Jesus ascended into heaven. There is a biblical way, and a biblical purpose for acquiring this skill. The path to obtaining hope includes tribulations, knowing that tribulation produces perseverance; and perseverance, character; and then character, hope. Going through difficult times helps you gain strength. As things come against you, surprise you, or disappoint you, hope based on past tribulations and difficulties catapults you into handling what's ahead so you can push through in a positive way.

In earlier chapters, I told the story of Tim and having built our dream house. Along with that dream house was a pretty substantial mortgage based on both our incomes. Even though I was working and contributed significantly to our monthly income, I had lost the person who was responsible to oversee our financial well-being in the family unit. As a banker, I knew the answer would be to refinance into a thirty-year note or obtain a lower interest rate. But I didn't qualify on just my income. This was also during the time I had quit my executive job and moved to Colorado when Levi was attending Charis Bible College. There was absolutely no way I could take on such a significant monthly payment, so I had rented out our house. I had found good tenants, but I was always thinking about the possibility of something going wrong. I didn't have enough reserves to handle any loss. We were upside down with the mortgage because of the 2008 recession, and like many executive homes at that time, there was a substantial drop in value.

It was highly stressful, and during that time I came to the end of myself. I realized I couldn't possibly oversee the house or guarantee that nothing would go wrong. I couldn't guarantee I would have a renter to cover the expenses. In fact, I was going backward, and certainly working at the phone center for $10 per hour wasn't going to pay a monthly mortgage. I had so much stacked against me, trying to take on this responsibility and figure out what to do by myself. I was headed for dire consequences, worrying about all that was involved. I was worn out, stressed out, and I had no choice but to give it to God. I had to let God know, "I can't do anything about this. I need You to take care of it." It was at that point when He probably said, "Phew! Finally, she gave up." I persevered through those difficult times, and it was miraculous. For eight years, I did not miss one payment, nothing was late, and just a few months ago, we were able to sell the home, yielding a substantial check at closing.

*Because I was faced with constant pressure in this area, I had to grow up. I had to find peace in every situation.*

Had I not learned to persevere in that situation and give everything to God to bring about hope for the future, I would have missed something special. During this period, I tried to sell the house multiple times, but God put on my heart the reason it wasn't selling—He would cause it to sell when it would benefit me most. That's exactly what happened.

How did that help me? Well, now when I'm facing a financial situation, purchasing property, facing a shortfall or starting a business, I'm able to tap into my experience, hold on to peace, and receive hope that God will see me through every situation. "Praying at all times in the Spirit, with all prayer and supplication. To that end, keep alert with all perseverance, making supplication for all the saints" (Eph. 6:18, ESV).

Persistence and perseverance will always work to your benefit. Through perseverance, I was also able to grab hold of my emotional maturity. It's exhausting to throw emotional fits—especially when they could be daily occurrences. Because I was faced with constant pressure in this area, I had to grow up. I had to find peace in every situation. So even though the financial pressure was intense, I kept it between the Lord and me, and He taught me to hang in there with Him. There were times I felt emotionally lost and gave in to fear, but He helped me stay steady amidst the pressure.

I tell you what, nothing works like the Word when going through difficulties. "You, however, have followed my teaching, my conduct, my aim in life, my faith, my patience, my love, my steadfastness" (2 Tim. 3:10, ESV). Difficulties are not brought on by God. Tim and I had made a decision to go into substantial debt with high payments, not knowing what was ahead of us. It was a decision we made, but even in that God was with us, and He helped me walk through it. Perseverance is important. It brings about hope, and it builds character that's necessary for success in all areas of life.

## ACTIVATION

Describe a meeting facilitated by an enthusiastic leader. How did it affect you and those around you?

List some habits you would like to start and some you would like to stop.

How do you speak to yourself and others? Is your self-talk positive or negative?

List some attributes that produce excellence. Do you see these attributes in yourself? In others?

List some qualities you have developed during rough times. Find promises in the Word for those who endure.

### Keys to Success Download:

https://drive.google.com/file/d/1jxDVPLQrmb58HBYZZF2DTxstmW0rmG Ie/view?usp=sharing

## Success Made Simple:

https://www.youtube.com/
playlist?list=PLuh1d30AgdvhVKKcGHDRm54PUAKCyS2KB

Chapter Nine

# How-to Tips to Reach Your Destiny

God has blessed me throughout my career with some amazing mentors. Some of my favorite mentors were Billy and Becky Epperhart with WealthBuilders. Even when I wasn't working directly for Billy and Becky, they took an interest in my success. They encouraged me at every opportunity, provided speaking opportunities at their events, and genuinely cared about me as a person. Through their mentorship, I learned about starting a successful business, how to build wealth, and how to trust God through challenges. I could never have attained the depth of their wisdom through traditional learning. I trust them as my mentors. Based on that earned trust, they can speak into my life in any area. I am open to listen and learn from them on any subject. Over the years, through their mentorship, I have "caught" wisdom and knowledge that was not available to me outside of my relationship with them. I can honestly say their mentorship has increased the quality of life in my career, family, and marriage. That is the power of a good mentor.

I have put together some valuable attributes for success that could also be considered learned behaviors. These five "How-to" tips can

Your emotions are not good or bad, they just are. Don't let them control your life.

be expanded in your life by utilizing mentorship alongside each one. Mentorship comes in various forms from purely observational, quite casual, or very formal. You can be mentored by your favorite speaker by observing, critiquing, and imitating. Also, you can be mentored by an admired colleague through observing, questioning, and shadowing. Or you can ask someone who is successful in your field to formally mentor you. This may include regular meeting times, sharing of ideas and strategies, and much more, based on mutual agreements and boundaries. You could choose one or more types of mentoring, but I highly recommend having a mentor related to your purpose. Mentorship is a valuable tool found in Scripture and utilized in many professions. As you read through this chapter, think about people you know who already do these things well. Then, begin to observe them and practice their methods.

## HOW TO SPEAK ON YOUR FEET

**Be ready any time to articulate and communicate effectively.**

Jesus had ready answers for true seekers, as well as hostile opponents. He set the precedent for His followers. You need to be ready to speak truth and wisdom in any given moment. The following Scripture describes a scene when the Pharisees intended to trap Jesus, but He turned it around with a ready answer full of wisdom.

"Then the Pharisees went and plotted how they might entangle Him in His talk. And they sent to Him their disciples with the

Herodians, saying, 'Teacher, we know that You are true, and teach the way of God in truth; nor do You care about anyone, for You do not regard the person of men. Tell us, therefore, what do You think? Is it lawful to pay taxes to Caesar, or not?' But Jesus perceived their wickedness, and said, 'Why do you test Me, you hypocrites? Show Me the tax money.' So they brought Him a denarius. And He said to them, 'Whose image and inscription is this?' They said to Him, 'Caesar's.' And He said to them, 'Render therefore to Caesar the things that are Caesar's, and to God the things that are God's'" (Matt. 22:15-21, NKJV).

Paul, one of the great champions of the faith, mastered the art of persuasion; he was always ready to debate, articulate, defend, and communicate effectively to lead people to truth. Jesus and Paul both sought the Father and were diligent students of their trade:

"And Paul entered, as he usually did, and for three Sabbaths he reasoned and argued with them from the Scriptures, explaining [them] and [quoting passages] setting forth and proving that it was necessary for the Christ to suffer and to rise from the dead, and saying, This Jesus, Whom I proclaim to you, is the Christ (the Messiah)" (Acts 17:2-3, AMPC).

Are there times when you are called on to speak or report unexpectedly and you freeze? It has definitely happened to me. Early on, I realized how often I was required to think fast and speak with clarity. I needed to be unconcerned what people would think of me and be willing to mess up in order to improve. I finally developed a speaking method I was most comfortable using. I would use note cards with just bullet points of the highlights I wanted to talk about.

I knew I needed to know my topic well enough to communicate in between those bullet points.

I learned this the hard way one night at a work event in Minnesota. It was "baptism by fire," and I remember it as if it were yesterday. The bank I worked at had been acquired by a larger organization, and for several months I worked on the conversion team with executive leadership before I was named the retail banking director. I was asked to speak at a formal dinner to the board of directors and shareholders, providing an update on our work and sharing the results of our efforts. This was a whole new level for me. I had never addressed such an accomplished group of people. Before I went up to speak, I was so scared I was shaking! I had my note cards in hand and was studying them intently.

One of my coworkers saw how nervous I was and came over to encourage me. He gave me some of the best advice I have ever received. He told me not to be nervous but to just talk about what I had implemented to bring results, what I knew we needed to do going forward, and let my enthusiasm and personality come through. You see, he had confidence from observing me day to day to know that I knew what I was doing. He was telling me to speak from my experience, from what I knew, and to what the group wanted to hear. It released me from a selfish perspective, where all I could think about was what people would think of me if I made a mistake in my speech. This changed my life. It also electrified and blessed the audience. I went from being fearful of what people would think of me to speaking on what I lived and breathed every day. All the pressure was removed!

# *Fill your heart with God's Word so it effortlessly overflows from your speech, and become masterful in your trade.*

I realized I don't ever want to talk or do a speech about something I don't know or haven't experienced personally. I've learned throughout the years to position myself in areas where I'm experienced. If I go to do a job or consult or teach, I develop my knowledge and experience in those areas to a level where, even if I don't know the exact answers, I know enough about the subject to converse knowledgeably and know where I can find more details if needed. If you're prepared to be an effective communicator on the spot, you will have an edge wherever you are.

Fill your heart with God's Word so it effortlessly overflows from your speech, and become masterful in your trade. "The good person out of the good treasure of his heart produces good, and the evil person out of his evil treasure produces evil, for out of the abundance of the heart his mouth speaks" (Luke 6:45, ESV).

## How to Handle Your Emotions

**Your emotions are not good or bad, they just are. Don't let them rule your life, decision making, or relationships.**

Have you been in a situation at work or in a relationship where you let your emotions run away? Then, looking back at the situation you thought, *If only I hadn't said that, or if only I had paused before I sent that email.* Emotions are given by God so you know there's a positive side to them. After all, happy is an emotion! Sometimes when you have emotions of anger or hurt, they are clues that you need to pay attention to and grab hold of the underlying root of those feelings. When you learn to handle negative emotions, your life becomes smoother.

"Let all bitterness and wrath and anger and clamor [perpetual animosity, resentment, strife, fault-finding] and slander be put away from you, along with every kind of malice [all spitefulness, verbal abuse, malevolence]" (Eph. 4:31, AMP).

*When you learn to handle negative emotions, your life becomes smoother.*

THE PROMISE OF PURPOSE

You can create an atmosphere in your home or workplace that is fearful, and people don't feel they can trust you. This is one of the things for me that's a challenge. Sometimes I have emotions that are tough for me to grab hold of. What is the key? I had to learn to see things through the lens of God's Word and the way God would see them. Proverbs 15:1-4 offers us some advice for dealing with our emotions:

"A soft answer turns away wrath, but a harsh word stirs up anger. The tongue of the wise uses knowledge rightly, but the mouth of fools pours forth foolishness. The eyes of the Lord are in every place, keeping watch on the evil and the good. A wholesome tongue is a tree of life, but perverseness in it breaks the spirit" (NKJV).

Recently I was working with my team on an upcoming event, and when I tested the links and looked at the posts on social media, my team members had not put the URL or the link in properly. So if someone wanted to attend this event, there was nowhere to purchase the ticket with the discount we were offering. I become frustrated by these things because I want work done with excellence. My job is marketing, and to make people aware of events is a major piece of that job. When I found that the link was broken or something was overlooked, my emotions started to rise and simmer just below the surface.

Thankfully, maturity and wisdom have taught me to keep those emotions intact and view them correctly. I was able to get all my thoughts out in an email, but before I sent it, I went back and reread it, realizing I was not very happy with it, so I softened the language. My emotional state while putting the email together had not been in a positive place. Thinking about the recipient during these times can help us consider how our words might affect that person. It's a lot easier to back up, soften things, even stop myself, and ask, "What is the worst thing that can happen with this?" Emotions can cause you to see things much bigger, worse, or more impactful than they really are. When you learn to handle your emotions, it helps you understand why you're feeling the way you are.

When God gives you people to steward—your children to parent or your husband or wife—He is entrusting that person into a relationship with you. You have a responsibility to care for and protect those under your leadership. If you're to become eligible for more responsibility, a larger organization, or more people reporting to you, one of the things required is to keep your emotions intact. Unhealthy emotions can cause issues in your place of work, in your home, or wherever you are. "Therefore see that you walk carefully [living life with honor, purpose, and courage; shunning those who tolerate and enable evil], not as the unwise, but as wise [sensible, intelligent, discerning people]" (Eph. 5:15, AMP).

## How to Handle Criticism

**It has no authority except what you give it.**

This one is a challenge, isn't it? We never enjoy having other people tell us what we're doing wrong. I like to think I do everything right, but in order to be successful, lead a business, grow your sphere of influence, or manage employees, it's important to learn how to handle criticism. There are two kinds of criticism—positive and negative. We must realize which type of criticism is coming our way and handle it appropriately. "If you listen to constructive criticism, you will be at home among the wise. If you reject discipline, you only harm yourself; but if you listen to correction, you grow in understanding. Fear of the Lord teaches wisdom; humility precedes honor" (Prov. 15:31-33, NLT).

*In order to be successful, lead a business, grow your sphere of influence, or manage employees, it's important to learn how to handle criticism.*

Let's talk about positive criticism, which is designed for your benefit. One of the first questions to ask yourself is, "Am I open to feedback? Am I open to someone suggesting a better way or recommending an adjustment?" To receive positive criticism, you need to trust the person giving the feedback: "It takes a grinding wheel to sharpen a blade, and so one person sharpens the character of another" (Prov. 27:17, TPT).

You can probably relate to situations that Dave and I find ourselves in once in a while as newlyweds. We were in our backyard a couple months ago, and I wanted to be helpful. I decided to empty our swimming pool scupper that was full of leaves. I had taken care of our pool in Minnesota and was accustomed to doing it a certain way. I was quite proud of myself for pitching in. As I began to remove the basket, Dave made an "observation" on how it should be done—oh yes, you know where this is going.

Apparently, there's a way to do it that keeps the leaves from getting into the pump. I was wondering why this wasn't a problem with my pool in Minnesota. I was only trying to help! It seems like a little thing, but my emotions registered from threatened to annoyed. Thoughts began flying madly. *What? Do you think I don't know anything? I've been doing just fine for longer than I can remember.* And on and on, spiraling down from there.

Knowing the heart of the person, along with his or her character and value shown for you, can help prepare you for feedback. I really didn't like what I was hearing, but I know my husband is all for me. Once you get straightened out in your thinking, you're able to hear the criticism or suggestion not as negative but positive. I realized that Dave just loves me so much, he wants me to be able to do this better. Matthew 18:15 tells us, "If your fellow believer sins against you, you must go to that one privately and attempt to resolve the matter. If he responds, your relationship is restored" (TPT). It's important how you handle suggestions and how you're able to view them. We need to remain open to positive criticism and feedback, which may require us to do things differently.

Now, contrast the above description with negative criticism. There are times when people give us feedback or criticism that's only meant to harm or mislead us. "And never let ugly or hateful words come from your mouth, but instead let your words become beautiful gifts that encourage others; do this by speaking words of grace to help them" (Eph. 4:29, TPT). This type of criticism you and I are not required to listen to or heed. If there's someone being critical of you—we have all experienced someone saying something untrue or unkind—bring it to the Lord in prayer. I will ask God if there's something I need to listen to, as much as it hurts. But when a person is carelessly saying something to hurt me, I have no obligation to consider it.

*Being able to handle criticism is crucial. Accept the positive, and set aside the negative.*

In this day of social media, people are quick to criticize and slow to consider consequences. If you're being criticized outside the boundaries of your well-being, just let it go. I hope this helps someone who has grown up thinking you have to consider every bit of criticism you hear, listen to it, and blame yourself. That is not the case. Determine if it is positive and if the person giving you feedback actually wants you to succeed and to help you, even if that person is pointing out something you did wrong or that you need to do differently. Or is it negative feedback from someone whose criticism is designed to hurt or discourage you and push you off track from what God has called you to do? Being able to handle criticism is crucial.

Remember, there are two kinds of criticism:

| **POSITIVE**<br>(constructive)<br>criticism—designed<br>for your benefit | **NEGATIVE**<br>(destructive)<br>criticism—designed<br>for your ruin |
|---|---|

Know the difference. Accept the positive, and set aside the negative.

## HOW TO CONQUER WORRY AND PRESSURE

**Working out of your purpose brings confidence and freedom from fear.**

Problems are an opportunity for success. I know that seems cliché, but it's a way for you to exercise faith in God. When problems show up, instead of worrying or stressing, you can be disciplined to give the situation to the Lord. Find Scriptures that minister to you in that area, and release it to Him. He is able to move in grace to solve issues and resolve problems.

Can you imagine getting to the point that every time a problem arises you say, "Yes! This is a great opportunity for me to work through my faith and see success." Well, that is God's will for us. "Let your heart be always guided by the peace of the Anointed One, who called you to peace as part of his one body. And always be thankful" (Col. 3:15, TPT).

There are two keys in this Scripture to avoiding stress and worry. First, ask the question, "Is this what I'm called to do? Is this my purpose, or have I wandered into something God never asked me to do?" If that's the case, no problem. Just seek Him on how to fulfill your commitment, and then get back on track with your purpose. But the other key here is to be thankful. When you express thanksgiving in the midst of trouble, you can know that God is going to bring peace. "They will not live in fear or dread of what may come, for their hearts are firm, ever secure in their faith. Steady and strong, they will not be afraid, but will calmly face their every foe until they all go down in defeat" (Ps. 112:7-8, TPT).

Your heart can be steadfast until you see His desire upon your enemies. Sometimes we think our enemies are people, but the Word says we don't fight against flesh and blood but powers, principalities, and the rulers of darkness. Enemies are anything that comes against your peace or ability to fulfill God's will. Your enemy might be a health issue, a challenge in your finances, a pattern of thinking, or your emotions. But this verse tells you to trust in the Lord and rest in Him, and you will be stable, steadfast, and see the Lord work on your behalf to overcome your enemies. Isn't that good news?

When I feel fear, stress, or anxiety, I remember this verse and speak it out loud, inserting my name: "For God has not given us a spirit of fear, but of power and of love and of a sound mind" (2 Tim. 1:7, NKJV). The Word of God is a weapon for us to use. We can speak it out. If I can't speak it out loud, I think and meditate on it. But when stress, fear, and worry come, you need to stand against it with the Word of God, seeing things through the lens of God's Word. Proverbs 3:5-6 tells us to "Trust in the Lord with all your heart, and lean not on your own understanding; in all your ways acknowledge Him, and He shall direct your paths" (NKJV). The word *direct* means "to make straight and right." This is a wonderful verse. If you're facing anything that's attempting to cause stress or anxiety in your life, trust in the Lord and lean not on your own understanding.

Leaning on your own understanding could include analyzing a situation in the natural, reading the news, or focusing on something negative. But it doesn't necessarily mean to disregard those things. It means don't base your decisions on them, and don't exalt those things over the promises of God. In all your ways, you are to acknowledge Him, and He shall direct your path. Even in the midst of something very difficult, you can say, "Lord, I'm stressed right now. I'm feeling anxiety and pressure. But I choose to acknowledge You and turn the situation over to You." I do this quite a lot.

*If God has promised it,*
*He will perform it on your behalf.*

I have learned this lesson over and over and over, especially when trying to make something grow. I release it to the Lord, after saying, "Is there anything else I can do?" He's more than happy to bring the increase. I also ask Him, "Is this going to be okay? Is there something I need to be concerned about here?" And almost every day He says, "It is going to be fine. Do not worry about it." I can hold on to that word from Him. I won't worry about it. I can put my faith toward it and take the pressure off of myself, putting it back on the Lord, who can handle the pressure and who will fulfill His promise. "And which of you by being anxious can add a single hour to his span of life?" (Matt. 6:27, ESV).

If you have something on your heart you've been worrying about, I want to encourage you that if God has promised it, He will perform it on your behalf. Everything good is from the Father, so just release it to Him. And you can even speak out loud, "Lord, I am releasing this to You, and I'm trusting You to bring about the results promised in the Word. I thank You and honor You for it. I'm going forward stress free."

## How to Be Decisive

**Sometimes any decision is better than no decision. Indecisive leadership is discouraging.**

Sometimes any decision is better than no decision. James tells us that a wavering or double-minded man will receive nothing from the Lord.

"My brethren, count it all joy when you fall into various trials, knowing that the testing of your faith produces patience. But let patience have its perfect work, that you may be perfect and complete, lacking nothing. If any of you lacks wisdom, let him ask of God, who gives to all liberally and without reproach, and it will be given to him. But let him ask in faith, with no doubting, for he who doubts is like a wave of the sea driven and tossed by the wind. For let not that man suppose that he will receive anything from the Lord; he is a double-minded man, unstable in all his ways" (James 1:2-8, NKJV).

# *If you don't give your team solid direction, it undermines their confidence in you and in themselves.*

There are times when you might doubt, but when you're decisive, you can trust the Lord with your decision. If I'm thinking about something and wondering, *Am I wrong? Am I right? I sought the Lord, and I felt this was the right direction to go, but now I'm not sure.* If I start wavering, where is my faith? It's in myself—my abilities to accomplish it on my own—and not in Him.

What if, as a leader, you have given your team a decision? You said, "Let's go in this direction," but then started wavering and waffling, being double minded. Your team members don't know what to do. If you don't give your team solid direction, it undermines their confidence in you and in themselves. They don't know what to do to be successful. In this situation, I believe that God doesn't have a pathway to come in and help you move forward. God doesn't call you to never make a mistake. He didn't say, "I'll bless you as long as you act perfectly," or "I'll give you favor and bring you increase as long as you never make a mistake in judgment." That's not what He says.

If you seek God and do the best you can, His grace is sufficient. He is able to steer a ship that is in motion. It will give those who look to you for leadership a decision to follow and be successful. Be decisive. Indecisive leadership is discouraging. Decisive leadership is encouraging and instills confidence in you and your team.

## ACTIVATION

Does your preparation time include studying God's Word and seeking His voice? Do you make time to learn more about your trade?

Practice harnessing your emotions. What is your EQ (Emotional Intelligence or Emotional Quotient)? Are you able to face challenges without responding emotionally to those around you?

Think of times you have had both positive and negative criticism. What were the results of each, and how could you have responded better to each?

Stress is simply worry or fear. How do you get rid of stress? How do you view problems?

Can you think of a time you had indecisive leadership? How did it make you feel? How did it affect those around you?

## Keys to Success Download:

https://drive.google.com/file/d/1jxDVPLQrmb58HBYZZF2DTxstmW0rmG
Ie/view?usp=sharing

## Success Made Simple:

https://www.youtube.com/
playlist?list=PLuh1d30AgdvhVKKcGHDRm54PUAKCyS2KB

# No one can stop you from being successful but you.

Chapter Ten

# Becoming Purposeful

During thirty-plus years of business, leadership, and consulting, I have learned a few things about success and failure. One key trait of success is the ability to execute a plan and implement the activities necessary to support it. Another is being purposeful in doing what is necessary to achieve the desired results. This applies to every area of our life.

Think about it. You could have an awesome God-given vision, a stack of creative ideas, even a beautifully documented strategic plan for your business, but nothing will happen unless and until you learn to effectively implement them. When I worked for MidCountry Bank in Minnesota as the Senior Vice President of Retail Banking, we created a program called Mining for Ideas. The program was designed to encourage our team members across the three states to share their ideas to improve operational efficiency, increase revenue and customer base, suggest new products and services, reduce losses, and more. It was also a way to provide employees with an opportunity to think outside the box, have a clear path to share ideas through the right channel, help us to improve as a department and organization, and have an opportunity to be recognized.

# We were purposeful from the start, and it paid off.

My team of leaders was really excited about the program we developed, but before I moved forward with rolling it out across the organization, I had some requirements. If we were going to start a program like this, asking for ideas from our team members, we had to commit to a disciplined, consistent process, which included: 1) reviewing the ideas every month at our monthly leaders' meeting; 2) clearly documenting the ideas submitted; 3) formally evaluating the ideas submitted; 4) acknowledging and publicly reporting back to the employees who had submitted ideas; 5) rewarding employees whose ideas were chosen; and 6) implementing the ideas chosen and reporting back on the results. If team members are asked for their input, providing an opportunity for people to voice their ideas and opinions, but there's no follow-up or way to communicate results, it's better to not ask for input at all.

We committed to the six steps listed above, and successfully launched and implemented Mining for Ideas across the organization. It was a tremendous success, yielding amazing results for the organization's bottom line and improving the morale and satisfaction of the employees who participated in the program. We were purposeful from the start, and it paid off.

When Dave and I got married, we took time to talk about and document our vision as a couple and family for the upcoming year. We discussed our priorities, things we wanted to accomplish, and goals we wanted to attain. Two items from the list of things that we agreed were important to us as a couple were staying fit and praying together. We knew that if we just listed our goals without making a realistic, actionable plan to accomplish them in our everyday lives, the year would pass, and we would not attain those goals.

We designed and committed to a daily schedule of exercise each morning—taking a walk together one day and doing a form of Pilates the next. Then, on Pilates day, we chose a Scripture from Grandma Esther's prayer box, talked about it, and prayed together based on that Scripture at the end of our workout. Even when we travel, we follow this schedule. At this point, it's a way of life. We have attained our goal of staying fit and praying together by being purposeful in how we start our day.

The following are five practical tools that will help you to become purposeful in every area of your life.

## BE A FINISHER

**Ideas without actions will not yield results. If you don't quit, you win. You are created to bring things to the finish line.**

Let's look first at the life of Jesus and all He did while on the earth. He is the best example for us of a finisher. "So when Jesus had received the sour wine, He said, 'It is finished!' And bowing His head, He gave up His spirit" (John 19:30, NKJV). Without the work Jesus did, we would be lost. Without all the suffering He went through, all the words He spoke, all the prayers He prayed, all the wisdom He poured into the disciples, God's plan would not have been fulfilled. He showed us the value of a completed work, which is to glorify God. "I glorified you on earth, having accomplished the work that you gave me to do. And now, Father, glorify me in your own presence with the glory that I had with you before the world existed" (John 17:4-5, ESV).

*No matter how much work I put into something, if I didn't finish it I would never reap the rewards of my efforts.*

When I was growing up, I loved doing craft projects. I would sit with my grandma, my mom, my aunts, and cousins on Sunday afternoon at my grandma's and do crafts. I was interested in all sorts of things: cross-stitching, sewing doll clothes, even learning to crochet and make quilts. I was a great starter, but finishing was a struggle for me. I would start on a project but never complete it, so I always had a box of unfinished crafts and sewing items. Maybe you can relate to this. None of my crafts were hung on the walls, and no quilts decorated my bed because I didn't finish any of them.

Looking back, it's kind of discouraging, but honestly it taught me a lesson. I realized that no matter how much work I put into something, if I didn't finish it I would never reap the rewards of my efforts. Luke 14:28 talks about this very thing: "For which of you, intending to build a tower, does not sit down first and count the cost, whether he has enough to finish it" (NKJV). Jesus says to count the cost. When you begin a project, a business, or something with your family, God says count the cost.

You can develop a process to help you finish what you've started. A process requires wisdom, knowledge, and thinking strategically on the front end. It requires asking questions, such as: Do you have enough money to complete the project? Do you have enough personal bandwidth? Do you need more team members? What will the finished project look like? In all your endeavors, the goal is to stand with Paul and be able to say, "I have fought the good fight, I have finished the race, I have kept the faith" (2 Tim. 4:7, ESV).

> ## THE LAW OF ATTRACTION AND FAVOR
>
> **You are an ambassador who gives people their first glimpse of Jesus. Take time to be favorable in appearance (dress and countenance), giving authenticity to what you carry.**

Expect the best. God has provided for you. His Word says that He has given us favor in the sight of God and man. Isn't that awesome? "A good man obtains favor from the Lord, but a man of wicked intentions He will condemn" (Prov. 12:2, NKJV). Have you ever walked into a room full of people to speak with or teach and started thinking, *What if they don't like me? What if they don't want to hear what I have to say? What if I get off the stage, and everyone is talking about how bad I was?* This kind of self-talk can make you nervous and doubtful of your call.

*God has given us the law of favor, but it's up to us to agree with that law and approach situations expecting the best.*

The understanding that God has provided favor helps you confidently approach a situation that you feel nervous about. If you go into the situation with your mind set on the thought that God has already given you favor, you can relax. There's a big contrast between doubting and the attitude of having favor. When you know you have favor with people—they like you, they're open to you and respect you—you'll get a much better result. God has given us the law of favor, but it's up to us to agree with that law and approach situations expecting the best.

This applies to every area of your life. All of these keys to success have a spiritual context based on the Word of God. There is a relational context, a work context, and also a financial context. When my expectation is favor in a situation, I can take it and lean into God for the results. This is such a stress-free way to live.

I have some questions for you: Do you look like what you carry? Do you look like you are carrying the love of Jesus? Do you look like you are prosperous in your business? Do you look like you are full of joy and full of peace? Doing so will help you bring the favor of God into conversations and situations to create an atmosphere that reflects His goodness and grace.

## KEEP FINANCIAL RESERVES

**Having a cushion to help weather bumps in the road is good stewardship.**

God has called you to be a good steward. He spends a lot of time in His Word talking about how to handle finances, such as in Proverbs 21:20: "There is precious treasure and oil in the house of the wise [who prepare for the future], but a short-sighted and foolish man swallows it up and wastes it" (AMP). Good stewardship is important because it helps you manage money, time, and resources, affecting every area of your life. But also, the Bible commands you to lay up an inheritance for your children and your children's children. "A good man leaves an inheritance to his children's children, and the wealth of the sinner is stored up for [the hands of] the righteous" (Prov. 13:22, AMP). When combined with His promises in Deuteronomy, we can learn a lot about finances from a spiritual perspective. "You shall remember the Lord your God, for it is he who gives you power to get wealth, that he may confirm his covenant that he swore to your fathers, as it is this day" (Deut. 8:18, ESV). God wants you and me to be well taken care of with our finances, along with having enough to establish His kingdom.

*Good stewardship is important because it helps you manage money, time, and resources, affecting every area of your life.*

From a natural perspective, what happens when we're not good stewards? Have you ever been in debt or had a large credit card balance, and all at once you realize how much interest you are paying each month? Have you outspent the amount of money you make? I have been in those situations, particularly when I was younger and didn't know about stewardship. Let me tell you, it is not a good place to be. The number one cause of failed marriages over the years is money issues. When we don't have the money to pay our bills, put food on the table, or buy the things we know we need to take care of our family, it is very stressful. When at all possible, have financial reserves to remove this stressor from your life and relationships.

## ASK QUESTIONS AND BE A LIFELONG LEARNER

Jesus is the best example of asking questions and leading the situation. Surround yourself with people who know more than you.

Surround yourself with people smarter than you, even though it's not a very fun thing to do. As a leader, you want to be the smartest one in the room. But ironically, to be a good leader you need to surround yourself with people who know more about their particular subject than you do. Asking questions such as, "What do you think? What are your thoughts about this? What do you think is best?" is an excellent way to end an email to your team. I may be leading the team, but I don't know everything, and I want to learn as well. I can't read enough books to expand the information I wish I had. I like to learn from others around me, so I ask questions.

Jesus was a master of asking questions. As a matter of fact, when you spend time with Him, He asks lots of questions: "What are you thinking here? How could you have responded differently? What does My Word say?" He helps me know what I'm thinking when I'm not sure. If you seek to understand, you are able to move forward and be a positive, proactive influence in whatever it is you are called to do. It's important to be willing to hear opinions that don't match your own. Sometimes as a leader that can be difficult, because we think we need to be right. If I'm asking questions and someone has an answer that disagrees with what I said, the best thing I can do is hear what that person is saying and measure it against what I know as a leader.

*If you seek to understand, you are able to move forward and be a positive, proactive influence in whatever it is you are called to do.*

As the leader, you make the final decision, just as parents take responsibility to make the final decisions for their children. When you have been given authority in your position to make decisions, you must own those decisions. It's in your best interests to learn as much as you can about anything that might impact a situation and be willing to hear people propose different options than what you initially saw. By asking questions and asking opinions of people who work with or for you, the frequency of making good decisions increases, as well as the success of your team or family.

"Before disaster the heart of a man is haughty *and* filled with self-importance, but humility comes before honor. He who answers before he hears [the facts]—it is folly and shame to him" (Prov. 18:12-13, AMP). I often catch myself speaking before pausing, mainly as a parent. Or, if I think I'm an expert in an area and someone comes to me with an idea different from mine, it's hard for me to hear what that person is saying. I have already decided that based on my experience and what I know, it needs to be a certain way. But if I take a moment and listen, even if I go with the original idea, I'm still able to hear a different view. I'm able to honor that person, show respect, and explain why we are making a decision to go a different way.

When you allow people to offer input and then ask them questions, you open up an opportunity to teach and expand their knowledge. Functioning with an attitude of, "What I think is right," will not help your team learn, plus it shuts down their creativity. When you exhibit the humility to re-examine some of the decisions you're making or the knowledge you have, even if you stay with the original decision, the Word of God says that is honorable. Humility comes before honor.

## YOU HAVE THE POWER OF CHOICE

**No one can stop you from being successful but you. Don't allow roadblocks or discouragement to have more power in your life than the Word. You are in charge of you.**

This goes against the grain of what you are being told in the secular media today. There's a big push to make you feel like a victim and blame someone else for the problems in your life. If the enemy is successful in selling you a victim mentality, telling you that you have no choice because everyone else is causing your life to be unsuccessful, you've lost hope. That is a miserable way to live, feeling as though you are powerless. God tells you He has given you power and authority on the earth. He also encourages you that no matter who you are, the promises of God are yes and amen: "For all the promises of God find their Yes in him. That is why it is through him that we utter our Amen to God for his glory" (2 Cor. 1:20, ESV).

The key is finding your identity in Jesus and who He says you are. Now, this doesn't mean you won't have challenges or ever be treated unfairly. But it does mean that if you see challenges through the lens of being a victor and not a victim, you'll be able to walk through any situation to the other side and see success.

*You are in charge of you.*

I want to encourage you that when you look at your life, realize you have the power of choice. My friend Robin was someone I worked with for twenty of my twenty-five-year career in banking, and as my boss he gave me rich wisdom over the years. He also mentored Levi during his high school years. After Levi's graduation, Robin took him out to lunch one day and said, "Levi, something you need to always remember is that you are in charge of you." That has stayed with Levi for many years now, but it also impacted me, as I realized how true it was. I would like to say that I can't do this or that because of someone else, but when it comes down to it, I am in charge of me, and you are in charge of you. One of the most important keys to success is to remember that you and I have the power of choice, and we can choose success.

## ACTIVATION

For the next week, take one of these principles and pray over it, then listen to the Lord and journal what He says.

### Success Made Simple:

https://www.youtube.com/
playlist?list=PLuh1d30AgdvhVKKcGHDRm54PUAKCyS2KB

Your success is imminent when you are pursuing God and His purpose.

Chapter Eleven

# Living Out Your Purpose Today

We all have a different story. Some of us started with an amazing family, a beautiful home, great parents, and a small-town upbringing. This was my story. Then there are others who didn't have such a great start. Maybe things were very difficult, a broken home, alcoholic parents, abandonment, or abuse. But an amazing thing about God is that no matter where we start, His plan for us is to finish strong and be successful.

I recently heard someone tell the story of Carol Burnett. I may be dating myself, but she was an amazing comedienne and a wonderful lady. However, her start was a rough one. Her parents were both alcoholics, so her grandma raised her. I learned, among other scarcities, she didn't have a decent light to read by. She had to sit in a small, dimly lit bathroom to find enough light for her studies. That's a difficult start, but looking at her life in later years, she was extremely successful. She made people laugh and had dedicated her life to blessing others through humor. No matter what your story is, whether you've had a great start or you've had great struggles, God wants you to be successful in living out your purpose.

# *Every opportunity for success I'm presented with also has the risk of failure.*

My idea of success and the things God put on my heart will be different from what God put on your heart, and that's okay. The Word of God tells us what success looks like to Him, and you can extend that into the calling you have in your business, your family, your marriage, and your personal development.

I've come to realize that every opportunity for success I'm presented with also has the risk of failure. The Father doesn't protect us from risk automatically because it would hinder us from the opportunity to be successful. He understands that we will make mistakes as we learn to walk in belief and trust, but those mistakes will bring about growth. Perhaps you can remember a time in your life when you tried something and failed. Despite failures, you are still loved and accepted by God. Hebrews 10:38 encourages us not to pull back or shrink in fear; God does not take pleasure in that. And Ephesians 1:6 says that you are made accepted in Jesus. You can rest assured that His love for you doesn't change with your successes or failures.

The Bible gives us the definition of success and failure. Success is persistence to accomplish a desired outcome no matter how long it takes. And failure is quitting before the desired outcome is reached. In Proverbs 24:16, we read, "For though a righteous man falls seven times, he will rise again" (ISV). It doesn't say that you do not fall. God looks on your heart, and when you persist in believing and acting upon His Word, you build on His sure foundation. In Hebrews, the writer says that Abraham was counted as righteous because he believed, even though at first he quit holding on to God's promise. Keep in mind on your way to becoming successful, you will likely experience some failures, but don't quit or give up!

Jesus made a success statement in John 17:4 that works for you and me: "I glorified you on earth, having accomplished the work that you gave me to do" (ESV). He lived His life in a way that brought glory and honor to His Father and accomplished all He was called to do. You receive your identity by faith, and you live out your life by grace, which is God's ability and power to enable you to do and be everything He says you can do and be. All of this is possible, as you see in Colossians 1:12, "Giving thanks to the Father, who has qualified us to share in the inheritance of the saints (God's people) in the Light" (AMP). You are qualified in God, and you live in the inheritance of Jesus. Realizing that your success is made possible through Jesus Christ (see Rom. 3:27), you can give Him the glory.

There will be times throughout your life when success will look different depending on your time and season of life. For example, in my twenties, with my first job out of college, I was just happy to have a job to be able to pay rent and buy a car without help from my dad. Success for me was moving into a position where I had some autonomy and some responsibility. Twenty years later that would not have looked like success to me. I was in a totally different season.

There was the season my son Levi was born. It was important for me to be a good mom, so an executive travel schedule wouldn't have looked like success when my primary responsibility was raising my son. Seasons change periodically, and it can be confusing, as we wonder, *Lord, am I missing You somehow?* Yet, something has begun stirring on the inside of you. You become a little uncomfortable—I call it holy discontent—because God wants to nudge you to the next level of success.

What season are you in? Are you in a season that's ending? Are you in a season that should've ended, but you're just hanging on because of the comfort level there? Or are you in a difficult season, and you're challenged to believe that God has anything good ahead for you? It could be a little of all these. Now that you've discovered your purpose, it's time to embrace that holy discontent and see where the Lord will take you.

But first things first. You need to have the Word of God as a foundation in your life. As you strive to follow the Word, you'll be able to grab hold of the Lord for strength. You'll grow through the comfort of the Holy Spirit, through Bible teachings, through sharing stories, and through learning from others' experiences. There are people currently in positions where you could conceivably be in two or three years. Ask questions, and learn how they got there. But above all, know that the foundation is the Word of God.

You won't complete anything in God's will without His help. That's part of being a child of God. He walks alongside you, and He wants to help you. Together, you will be able to achieve success at a much higher level than you could dream or do on your own. That's part of the fun and the adventure of walking with the Lord. You may say, "Alright, I'm ready! I want a new season, and I'm going to the next level of success." Remember, it all starts with your heart-to-heart, living, vibrant relationship with the Savior of the world.

# God has created you uniquely based on the gifts and talents He's given you.

When I discovered my purpose, my life catapulted. All areas of my life took off once I had an understanding of my purpose in the Lord. Anything I considered success in the past paled compared to living out my purpose through Him. I'm not talking about my purpose being a job or a position but how He designed me—how I approach work that makes the best use of His gifts and talents. It also brings me the most joy and protects me from finding my identity in performance or other people's opinions. I have been freed from man's approval. There are a lot of things you can do to remove the fear of man from your life. One of the most effective ways is to know what God has designed you to do and for what purpose He's created you.

God has made you special. He's created you and me as individuals unlike anyone else. The world tries to get you to think that being successful means looking like a movie star or a model. But God has created you uniquely based on the gifts and talents He's given you. Be free from looking at other people and comparing your success and failure with theirs. God has given them a different purpose than

He has given you. Your greatest success in life is to strive after His righteousness and His way of doing and being right. Then you can be assured you're doing the things needed for the purpose God has designed specifically for you.

What happens when the Lord gives you an idea of how He wants you to move forward with your purpose? What happens when you say yes to an invitation to join in an adventure and assignment with God? Here are just some of the things you can expect to receive from Him: His glory, favor, power, authority, wisdom, divine appointments, and open doors. I love God's open doors and not the doors that I have to pound and push through to get to an opportunity.

You can also expect God's grace because it won't be done in your own strength. And there will be God's anointing, passion, and pruning in your life. You might say that all that sounds good, except the pruning—what's with that? Pruning is good as well. It's necessary to be able to grow in the spirit, in the natural, in the kingdom, and in your relationship with the Lord. Jesus says that pruning is for your good and to increase your fruitfulness. That's what we want in this life. We want to produce fruit for the Lord.

Jesus provided the explanation for the pruning work in our lives in John 15:1-3: "I am the true vine, and my Father is the vinedresser. Every branch in me that does not bear fruit he takes away, and every branch that does bear fruit he prunes, that it may bear more fruit. Already you are clean because of the word that I have spoken to you" (ESV). As God gently and lovingly prunes, you become more fruitful, and your true beauty comes out! The pruning process starts with God communicating in a kind, loving, and compassionate way about something He wants to adjust, such as an attitude or opinion. In response, your willingness to repent, or change your thinking, and obey takes you to the next step in your destiny. You can trust anything that He wants to prune in you is going to be good for you and will get you where you want to be!

Most often when you get an idea from God, you don't feel equipped to take it on. Have you experienced that? The Lord will put something on your heart and you think, *Are You talking to someone else? Because the skills and talents, all the things required for this, I feel like I don't have.* I'll tell you that's the perfect place for the Lord to bring you an assignment. He's not going to give you something you can do without any effort and without leaning into Him. That's exactly how I felt when the Lord impressed me to start a home staging business. I had no formal training and had never staged a home in my life! Yet this job sustained me financially while in Colorado.

*When He puts something on your heart that seems scary, remember God is the God of the impossible.*

Remember, this is an adventure together with God. So if you've received an assignment, and you feel totally ill equipped to carry it out, that's probably a pretty good sign the Lord is in it. If you receive something you can accomplish easily without any assistance or seeking the Lord, you might want to go back and be sure it was something He put on your heart. It could be something that you decided on your own would be a good next step.

God wants to be involved with you, and one of the special things about being a child of God is access to the wisdom of God. He says He'll give you wisdom when you ask Him for it. He gives it to you liberally and ungrudgingly (see James 1:5). When He puts something on your heart that seems scary, remember God is the God of the impossible. As you walk with Him through the process, it will come to pass. The Lord will bring success! Allow yourself time to grow in wisdom, which is the application of truth. Jesus didn't immediately know everything about Himself, His Father, or His ministry. Luke 2:52 says, "And Jesus increased in wisdom (in broad and full understanding) and in stature and years, and in favor with God and man" (AMPC). Just as Jesus grew in wisdom and in favor, you can also grow in favor and wisdom.

I have highlighted some things that God provides to help you feel equipped to move forward. These are all things that He gives you, but you must embrace and expand them as you partner with Him for your purpose.

## PASSION FOR GOD

Any venture you go into will hit a rough patch at some point. I'm not speaking negatively and without faith, but I'm saying that life has challenges. Difficulties help you grow, but God doesn't bring challenges to harm you. A passion for the Lord gets you through hardships, knowing that He has called you. You can look to Him to bring resolution and to give you strength. Often, He provides an idea or a way to do something you hadn't thought of before.

> *A passion for the Lord gets you through hardships, knowing that He has called you.*

When you hit rough patches or challenges, sometimes you're tempted to go back and question if you heard God. But if you address the doubt and have confidence in your relationship with the Lord and His calling, you won't give up. God knows your heart, so if you've got a big assignment and you just want to give up, don't worry about it. Go to the Lord and let Him know how you're feeling. Trust Him to infuse you with strength and passion and purpose for what He's called you to do. We all have moments when we don't feel equipped. We all have moments when we feel like giving up, but we can't be ruled by feelings. Hold on to the passion He's given you toward Him and your purpose.

## KNOWLEDGE, SKILL, AND ABILITY

When God gives you a big assignment, you're going to have to work to gain knowledge and skills to carry it out. Sometimes that's done in a supernatural way, where God gives you a talent you didn't know you had. Through being obedient in accepting the assignment, that new talent begins to show, and you end up with wisdom and abilities you didn't know you had. You'll receive knowledge that you didn't go to school to achieve. People around you begin to ask, "How did you see this? How do you know to do this?" And you realize that your ability isn't normal. It must be from God.

*Educate yourself to become a master in your field, whatever it is He has given you.*

There are also times when you grow in knowledge through good old-fashioned study and hard work. For instance, you'll learn how much you should charge, what your costs will be, if you need to staff people, and so forth. You'll need to develop this type of practical knowledge in order to be successful in your purpose, whether it is business, ministry, or home. Educate yourself to become a master in your field, whatever it is He has given you.

## CHARACTER AND ECONOMIC CAPACITY

Your character is linked to your economic capacity and is an area in which you need continual growth. Character is one of those things the Lord works in you. There's a saying that you're only as good as your name. I remember when I was growing up, both of my parents had great character. My dad was a businessman and CEO of a bank in a small town. Because he had such great character, when people found out I was his daughter, everything changed. I could ride on his name because he was a man of character, and people knew that. When I said my name was Karen Kruse, people would say, "Oh, you're Larry and Betty's daughter." The character and reputation my dad had built was available to me as well. As an adult, you have your own character and reputation to build. Then when your name comes up, it speaks something to people. Proverbs 22:1 describes a person's reputation and how the resulting favor on that person's life is more valuable than riches.

*Your character helps determine your economic capacity to be able to handle wealth.*

Character is important in economic capacity. There are two things to consider here. Economic capacity certainly means we have the funds to carry out the assignment God has given us. But the other part is closely aligned with character and determines the economic capacity you personally can sustain. Does your character make you safe for money and wealth? Money itself doesn't have power, but it amplifies what's in your heart. What you do with money brings power and influence in the natural. It's a reflection and accentuates what's on the inside of you. Your character helps determine your economic capacity to be able to handle wealth. And the more you're able to handle wealth from a character perspective, the more you can be entrusted with riches to expand the kingdom.

Deuteronomy 8:18 says that God gives you the power to create wealth that He might confirm His covenant, which He made with the fathers of our faith that you and I have access to. "But you shall [earnestly] remember the Lord your God, for it is He Who gives you power to get wealth, that He may establish His covenant which He swore to your fathers, as it is this day" (AMPC).

*God gives you ideas and insights for how to create wealth, and He provides knowledge and wisdom needed to see it manifested in our lives.*

Let's take a closer look at the verse to understand this relational blessing. God is the giver. He is our source, and it all flows from a relationship with Him. Power flows out of that relationship. Power is the strength, force, means, substance, and capacity—whether that's physical, mental, or spiritual—necessary to obtain wealth. This wealth includes resources, riches, substance, and influence. God gives us this power so that He may confirm His covenant. Material blessings are included in the promises to the patriarchs and to you and me as their descendants. In addition, you are a joint heir in Christ and have all blessings. God empowers you to create wealth to demonstrate His covenant, and influence is key to expanding His kingdom.

God gives you ideas and insights for how to create wealth, and He provides knowledge and wisdom needed to see it manifested in our lives. Proverbs 2:6-7 says, "For the Lord gives [skillful and godly] wisdom; from His mouth come knowledge and understanding. He stores away sound wisdom for the righteous [those who are in right standing with Him]; He is a shield to those who walk in integrity [those of honorable character and moral courage]" (AMP). I love how encouraging this passage is. The Lord has wisdom and ideas for you, and His wisdom is stored up for you.

When you walk honorably and in integrity, the Lord says He's your protection. You can go boldly into the areas of your purpose, knowing He has called you and given you wisdom. He's given you knowledge, and as you walk in His character, He'll protect you every step of the way. Isn't this amazing? That's encouraging because sometimes you'll have to take risks.

In the natural, when you take on an assignment or the Lord has put something on your heart without you knowing all the pieces, it can be risky. When you know that He's committed to be your shield, and He's stored up wisdom for you, then you can go boldly into that assignment with the confidence that you'll be successful.

Pick your dream up and let the Lord know you're excited to get moving forward. You are equipped to launch into success. And the purpose you were created for is right around the corner. You are equipped to step out into your destiny. Praise God!

## ACTIVATION

Think about how you handle change. Are you open to hearing the Lord for direction and leadership?

Do you consider pruning positive or negative? Why?

What are some of the pruning words of adjustment the Holy Spirit has spoken to you and the impact they have had on your life?

Ask the Lord to increase your passion for Him. Seek Him for areas of knowledge, skill, and ability where you need training. Discuss with a colleague or other safe person how he or she views your character, and ask the Lord if you are a safe place for money.

Ask the Lord if there are any dreams or visions that He gave you for your life that you discounted or didn't follow through on. Write them down as He brings them to your remembrance. Pray over them, and ask God to help you unleash your destiny.

## Launch into Success Free Download:

https://drive.google.com/file/d/1zkmXfjg_Dyag9d1jnyEZ2eGFdLcVuiTl/view?usp=sharing

# Conclusion

It is through God's purpose that you can achieve anything. "For the vision is yet for an appointed time; but at the end it will speak, and it will not lie. Though it tarries, wait for it; because it will surely come, it will not tarry" (Hab. 2:3, NKJV). If you feel it is too late to pursue God's purpose, let this Scripture encourage you. If you have dreams God has given you, but they have not yet been fulfilled, they will come to pass. When you are discouraged or don't see forward movement, God says there is an appointed time. God has a plan for your life. Dig in deep today and ask what He has for you. Tell the Lord, "I am going to trust You. I am going to pull those dreams out again and ask for help to move forward. I know Your plan for my life includes joy and success." You are created for an amazing purpose, and you have been supplied with the gifts and talents to achieve it. These truths are life changing. Grab hold of them and begin to live a life filled with purpose. You can expect to live in freedom, wealth, and perpetual fulfillment all the days of your life.

God is your entire source. He provides, not only your purpose, but everything you need to fulfill it. He is the source of the seeds you plant and the fruit you harvest. You can rest in His provision.

"So you shall keep the commandments of the Lord your God, to walk in His ways and [reverently] fear Him. For the Lord your God is bringing you into a good land, a land of brooks of water, of fountains and springs, flowing forth in valleys and hills; a land of wheat and barley, and vines and fig trees and pomegranates, a land of olive trees and honey; a land in which you shall eat food without shortage and lack nothing in it; a land whose stones are iron and out of whose hills you can dig copper. When you have eaten and are full, then you shall bless the Lord your God for all the good land which He has given you" (Deut. 8:6-10, AMPC).

God has brought you into this good land, and all these good things are yours. He is the One who brings harvest and wealth. God sees everything and He fulfills His Word. Keep your focus on Him and be a good steward of the gifts He has given you. Be a vessel for His ideas to flow through, then give Him the glory. Keep learning, seeking, and growing. There is so much available to you. "You shall remember the Lord your God, for it is he who gives you power to get wealth, that he may confirm his covenant that he swore to your fathers, as it is this day" (Deut. 8:18, ESV).

Commit to consistently turn your decisions over to the Lord. One of my most frequent prayers sounds like this: "Lord, if this is Your idea, I don't need to convince others. I ask You to speak to them and show Yourself faithful." This removes so much pressure. For this reason when measuring success, it doesn't matter who gets the credit. The harvest is coming from the Lord. There is great freedom in this. When you live for Him, God can do amazing things. Selflessly contribute your gifts and talents where He directs you. Steward those gifts and always give God the glory. Surround yourself with people who pour into your purpose. Find people who have so much vision it spills out over you. People who expect great things from God will help expand your vision. Get around people who will contribute to God's big vision for your life.

"And the Lord answered me: 'Write the vision; make it plain on tablets, so he may run who reads it'" (Hab. 2:2, ESV). What is your purpose? Write it down. He says make it plain so you can run with it. Let me encourage you in your purpose. Include your family, your work, and your dreams. God has plans of joy and success in every area of your life.

I hope this book has been an encouragement and a catalyst for you. Please use the individual pieces of this book to periodically refresh your heart on your journey to a life filled with purpose. Whether you have known your purpose for years or you discovered it while reading this book, I pray for life and joy and peace over you.

I would love to hear from you. Please email me at info@ karenconrad.net with your stories of victory and hope. Also, feel free to ask questions and share suggestions. For more resources, please take advantage of the links listed at the end of each chapter. May God richly bless all you set your hand to accomplish. Amen.

If you do not know God personally and would like to start a relationship with Him, you may do that right now. You can say something like the following in your heart or with words: "Dear Jesus, thank You for forgiving me. Come into my life (heart), and I'll follow You." Those words are usually known as a prayer of salvation, and by saying it, you receive the free gift of eternal life and the forgiveness of any wrongdoing. If you have said the prayer, you have started a relationship with God. If you did say this prayer for the first time, please email me at info@karenconradministries.net so I can be one of the first to welcome you into God's eternal kingdom!

# About Karen Conrad

KAREN CONRAD is a compelling communicator and strategist with a 30-year background in banking and consulting. She is the founder and director of Karen Conrad Enterprises, a strategic consulting and communication company for businesses and nonprofits. Her clients are represented by CEOs and entrepreneurs who implement her systems to increase profit and growth for their organizations. She is widely known for her innovative process "Vision to Reality," which guides individuals in discovering their purpose and achieving their full potential. She and her husband, Dave, happily reside in Dallas, Texas, and enjoy traveling together and investing quality time in their children and grandchildren.

# *Promise* JOURNAL

THE PROMISE OF PURPOSE

PROMISE JOURNAL

# The Harrison House Vision

Proclaiming the truth and the power
of the Gospel of Jesus Christ with excellence.
Challenging Christians
to live victoriously,
grow spiritually,
know God intimately.

Connect with us on